THRIVE

The Biblical Essential of Conquering Trauma and Being Resilient

Stephen K. Moore

WORKBOOK PRESS LLC
187 E Warm Springs Rd,
Suite B285, Las Vegas, NV 89119, USA

Website: https://workbookpress.com/
Hotline: 1-888-818-4856
Email: admin@workbookpress.com

Ordering Information:
Quantity sales. Special discounts are available on quantity purchases by corporations, associations, and others.
For details, contact the publisher at the address above.

ISBN-13:   978-1-954753-26-6 (Paperback Version)

REV. DATE: 01/07/2022

Thrive: The Biblical Essential of Conquering Trauma and Being Resilient

Stephen K. Moore

To my lovely wife Anita – Thank you for the many mornings of argument on the topic of Job and supporting me in the writing of this book.

TABLE OF CONTENTS

Introduction   I

Part I – Satan's Wager

    Chapter 1 – The Wager   1

    Chapter 2 – Satan Attacks   6

    Chapter 3 – Curses   11

    Chapter 4 – Without Reason   23

    Chapter 5 – Too Wonderful   32

    Chapter 6 – Verdict   48

    Chapter 7 – Unpacking   60

Part II – Faith Lessons for Daily Living

    Chapter 8 – The Unnamed   84

    Chapter 9 – Always Defend   99

    Chapter 10 – Memorials   123

    Chapter 11 – What Friends Do   134

    Chapter 12 – The Story of Job is About…   144

Epilogue   163

About the Author   170

PREFACE: THE UNEXPECTED FEEDBACK

"Your book got me through an impossible time."

That was a somewhat unexpected response to the book, *Satan's Wager: What the Devil and Job Got Wrong about God.* But then, as I shared in the first edition, over the years I found myself using the story of Job in unexpected ways.

The story of the suffering man found its way into marriage counseling, spiritual growth talks, and even just discussions about the challenges of everyday life.

But then, the Word of God *is powerful.*

From the feedback I received, I perceived the book needed to be rewritten and *re-titled* for the second edition. The people who were struggling with God due to severe illness, trauma and other challenges in their lives recommended that I title the book more along the truth of what it imparts—the secret that Job discovers can impart to us the ability to live tenaciously in traumatic times.

The story of Job in all of his incredible loss—imparts a vital *truth* on not just enduring hard times, but actually experiencing wonder and strength during them.

We live in a time in the Western world when people are more depressed, anxious, sleep deprived, morbidly obese, addicted, lonely, and suicidal than ever.

We live in a time when the Western world is missing the one key element that can endow us with strength and tenacity beyond measure—if we will quiet ourselves and listen deeply to the boil-covered man on the ash-heap.

Or perhaps better, to *watch* him in our mind's eye.

For at the most surprising time for a man who lost pretty much everything in an unimaginable attack—Job finds *wonder.*

Would you like to become unbreakable in trial? Would you like to kick old traumas to the curb? Would you like to face a very uncertain future not with dread or fear, but with wonder?

Do you want to *thrive?*

Then read on.

Join me around the ash heap with Job and his friends.

INTRODUCTION: THE AMAZING MISSED MESSAGE OF JOB?

I heard a preacher with a booming deep voice skillfully say, "The book of Job is about the problem of suffering."

You may have heard people exclaim when facing tough times, "Well, I'm no Job!"

Or you may have read a commentary comments such as, "Here [in the book of Job] is revealed the manner in which a righteous man should accept disaster."[1]

You know something? There is some truth in all of these comments. The story definitely involves suffering, and we can learn a lot about handling pain through reading it. And certainly, many if not all of us would doubt our ability to handle the incredible grief Job did in the manner he demonstrated. And perhaps the story does show us something in the way a righteous person should accept disaster – although maybe it shows us more than what we have ever understood.

But what if there is something much greater, something more powerful, something life changing for every person to be found in this ancient text?

What if suffering is *not* the primary topic?

What if the hero of the book is *not* Job, but someone else entirely?

What if understanding the story of this ancient battle between the God of Creation and a fallen created being more fully could revolutionize our daily walk with God?

What if the story of Job is one of the most under-appreciated and misunderstood messages in all of Scripture?

That's what *Thrive* contends. There lies buried in this amazing and grueling story a set of truths so profound that they are hard to grasp – but once grasped, they can transform your daily life. Want to know what these life-changing truths are? Keep reading.

What's Next

The first section of the book deals with the wager of Satan directly, what it was, the attack on Job, and whether or not Satan won the bet. Chapter 7 reveals the essential that allowed Job, and will allow you, to experience *wonder* in the midst of your worse days.

The second section deals with some of the other powerful faith-building takeaways to be found in the various characters and events of the story. Understanding these will allow you to face an uncertain future with confidence and laughter.

Brace yourself; you may have never seen this ancient story in this light before!

CHAPTER 1

THE WAGER

"...Reach out and take away everything he has, and he will surely curse you to your face!"[2]

Satan had shown up in the presence of the Almighty. The Almighty greeted him with a calm question; "From where have you come?"[3]

Satan's answer is challenging, it has always struck me in tone as what my English friends would call "cheeky." Some might call it arrogant or boastful, but this created being who rebelled against our (and his) Creator seems to be bragging a bit when he states, "From going to and fro on the earth, and from walking up and down on it."[4]

This is just a personal attempt to paraphrase the intent, but it seems that our Adversary is saying, "You know that beautiful earth you made and all those people you put on it? Well, I've been down there doing as I please. I've been wrecking the place!"

I say that only because Satan's response to The Almighty's next calm question seems so over-the-top and emotional. The one true God asks Satan, after his bragging claim about what he had been up to, "Have you considered my servant Job..."[5] and goes on to detail the faithfulness and service of the man. This seems to infuriate Satan – he is obviously well familiar with Job. That is one guy he *has not been able to wreck*. But he has an idea as to why Job is so dedicated:

Yes, but Job has good reason to fear God. You have always put a wall of protection around him and his home and his property. You have made him prosper in everything he does. Look how rich he is![6]

Do you understand what he is claiming? He is in effect saying that the only reason why someone would serve God faithfully is because of the benefits.

Not because The Almighty is worthy in and of himself.

Not because The LORD is mighty in grace and love.

Not because The LORD is the source of our being and of everything good.

No, Satan is standing before the Creator of all, including his own treasonous self, claiming that the only possible reason someone would be loyal to God would be because of the benefit package. In effect, Satan is defending his own actions of rebellion against God. But then he takes it up a notch.

Satan's Wager

It's bold. It is a direct challenge to The Almighty:

But reach out and take away everything he has, and he will surely curse you to your face![7]

Implied in this evil proposition is a premise. Satan had previously made the claim that the only reason why a man would be loyal to God would be because of the benefits. He states directly that it is only because of God's protection and giving of wealth that Job loves and serves Him.

Also implied in this statement is a statement about the love of God.

God protects and blesses someone, and they will serve him.

If God removes the blessing and protection, the creature will curse God, *and then...*

It is the "and then" that constitutes Satan's reward if and when Job does curse God. Isn't the Devil contending that while Job is faithful to God then he belongs to God; but if Satan can cause Job to curse God, then God will cast him away?

While the 18th Century Bible commentator Matthew Henry pointed out that Satan's challenge is a "censure"[8] of Job and this constitutes slander – consider more importantly what this wager says about God Himself; God may save you, but if you just happen to *curse* him, he'll cast you off. In other words, with God you are always on the short-leash. Your status with God is always hanging by the thinnest thread, because if you just happen to have a few bad days and say something bad about him, he will ditch you.

In years past the doctrine of grace was explained by some as "once saved, always saved." According to Satan's wager, the truth was, "If saved, *barely saved!*"

Satan is not only claiming that Job is weak and that his loyalty has been bought by God, but he is slandering the character of God even more. He is claiming that the Creator is the master of the performance-based relationship. Lucifer is saying that The One True God is very punitive in nature. He is willing to save, but he is sitting eagerly on his throne just waiting for you to – wait for it – curse him. Then you're a goner.

Satan Was Not Alone in this View

If you have studied Job before, you know where this is going. Satan is not alone in holding a low, punitive view of The Almighty. *Job strongly held this view as well.*

The first part of Job's story gives a three-sentence overview of who Job is[9] - it tells about where he lives, his family, his character, and his wealth. But then it launches into a rather peculiar tendency of Job regarding his adult children and their relationship with the Lord:

His sons used to go and hold a feast in the house of each one on his day, and they would send and invite their three sisters to eat and drink with them. And when the days of the feast had run their course, Job would send and consecrate them, and he would rise early in the morning and offer burnt offerings according to the number of them all. For Job said, "It may be that my children have sinned, and cursed God in their hearts." Thus Job did continually"[10]

Some of us have adult children just as Job did; I know when my kids call me or post a photo on social media when they are hanging out with each other it brings me great joy. It feels as though I at least did something right in raising them, in that they still have warm feelings of love toward one another and still *want* to be together. After years of the typical conflict and sibling rivalry of the younger years, seeing your adult children enjoying time together warms the heart.

But for Job, this was not entirely the case. He would "continually"[11] experience fear and eagerly anticipate the end of his children's time together. And once it was over, he would "rise early"[12] and start slaughtering animals to ease his great fear that something had occurred by accident while his children were together.

What was this fear? Why did something that would bring many parents joy cause such worry and even bloodshed (of Job's flocks) the morning after? It was this:

It may be that my children have sinned, and cursed God in their hearts.[13]

Job and Satan shared the same understanding of the character of God.

The Almighty, the one for whom Job lived every day and who was the driving force behind his righteousness was just sitting in heaven with a critical eye watching the secret thoughts of Job's children as they ate and enjoyed each other. In spite of Job's long relationship with his Creator, Job was convicted that the One he served was just waiting to catch one of his beloved children thinking a wrong thought – and then it would be all over for them. If in the gaiety of the occasion one of his children accidently said something bad about God, the Lord would certainly cast them away. There seem to be an expectation that punishment would be swift and irrevocable.

Job and Satan were not alone in their view either.

Curse God and Die

We are jumping forward in the story here, but we must in order to understand how common Satan's view of the nature of God was. Once Satan had brutally stripped Job of his wealth and health, Job's wife makes her cameo appearance on the scene.

Job at this point is covered in boils from his head to his toes. He is sitting on a burn pile using broken pottery pieces to scrape his boils open to drain the puss. This once great man now hardly resembles a man at all.

It is too much for his wife. Although nothing is said of the nature of her relationship with her famous husband, I suspect that someone with the servant heart of Job (as demonstrated by testimonies throughout the story, including that of The Almighty Himself) would have been a great lover in the truest and most meaningful sense of the word.

Their ten children likely indicate a warm and passionate physical relationship, and his concern for everyone from widows and orphans to strangers indicate that Job was the kind of person who put others above himself in all cases. So just in doing a bit of detective work, I would suspect that Job's wife genuinely loved the man dearly who had truly and faithfully loved her through their long years together.

And so, on that day when the shell of a man that used to be such a great man sat on the burn pile and scraped his boils, it was too much for her. It hurt her heart to see someone she loved so deeply in such a miserable and unrecognizable state.

Plus, often overlooked in this discussion, she had lost all ten of her precious children. These individuals whom had come from her body, that she had nursed at her breasts, and that had occupied her days for decades, were cruelly crushed in one horrendous gust of wind.

She was grieving, and when she went to her hero – the one she always went to for help – he was not in any condition to hold her and comfort her. It was more than she could stand. She likely felt that given the rapidness and ugliness of his decline that he was going to die, and so she expressed more clearly than either Satan or Job her understanding of the way God worked:

Curse God and die.[14]

There we have it. In her overwhelming grief, she blurted out what Satan and Job would not say with such clarity. In effect the belief of Job, his wife, and Satan was:

God may be great, he is the Lord of all, but don't dare say anything bad about him, because in the moment you do, he'll take you out.

And this is, I perceive, the reward implied in Satan's wager: What Satan understood to be the case was that if he was able to get Job to curse God, the Job would become *his possession*. It was a cosmic night at the gaming tables for Satan. He himself had rebelled as a created being and been expelled from the presence of God, permanently. He had a lot of experience since then with the little creatures that God put on the earth – he knew how to get under their skin and draw them away. He was desperate to humiliate his Creator by pulling this loyal and good man away – just as he had done so many times before with so many others.

Or at least that was the perception of Satan.

God accepts the wager, but Satan perhaps didn't fully catch what God said in the process – more on that later.

Why Satan's Wager Matters to You

If we examine the story more closely, even Job's friends (except for one) also shared this belief about a short-fused and ill-tempered God. And they are not alone either.

This view is still carried by many of us. I lived the first three decades of my life under this concept of God. After a brief stint as an atheist I returned broken and empty to the Lord of Lords. I was determined to do my best to make up for my arrogant rebellion. Yet I lived in fear that even one or two mistakes would cost me my place with God – for eternity.

And so for many of us, we can sing songs about God's love for us, Jesus' amazing sacrifice on our behalf, and hold some pretty impressive sounding spiritual dialogues about the limitless love of God. Yet in our deepest places, we fear that we just aren't good enough. We suspect that God is angry or disappointed with us. We fear that in a weak moment we might do just exactly what Job feared one of his children would do – curse God.

And then we would be cast away forever.

And so the outcome of Satan's wager is vitally important to our faith. It is crucial to understand what the result of the torture Satan imposed on Job actually was.

This is where the story often gets muddy though. Many readers over the years have operated from the assumption that Satan made the wager, tested Job, and Job passed. Therefore, God won the wager.

But is that the case?

We must first answer the question:

Did Job curse God?

This will take a few chapters to flesh out. Things are about to get ugly. And then they get even uglier.

CHAPTER 2

SATAN ATTACKS

Have I any pleasure in the death of the wicked, declares the Lord God, and not rather that he should turn from his way and live?[15]

When God finished creating the world, he stated that it was "very good."[16] Our Creator finds joy in making objects of beauty and purpose, and He loves His creation! As noted in the introductory Scripture above, contrary to what many believe, God does *not* desire the death of wicked people – He *truly* loves His creation. He loves *every single one of us!*

The ugly wager of Satan completely flies in the face of the desires of the One on the throne – and yet He goes along with it. Just as much as Satan desires to win his wager, God has a purpose of His own in permitting what is about to happen.

Satan is permitted to show much more of his true nature than is usual in the world. In two separate attacks, he faces few constraints in showing who he truly is.

Job's Suffering was Great – The First Losses

In case you are not familiar with the details, or if you are, it is instructive to review what happened to Job at the hand of Satan.

On one day, he lost 7,000 sheep, 3,000 camels, 500 yoke of oxen, 500 female donkeys, and very many servants. Think about how much land and structures would have been required to support this number of animals! This guy was loaded with the assets of his time.

To put it in modern terms, when he lost all of this in one day, it would be similar to a multi-billionaire losing all of his investments, cash, primary home, vacation home, vehicles and retirement funds in one day.

Each loss, such as the fire that consumed all of the sheep in one moment of time, was so dramatic that even the servant who observed the burning sheep recognized the source of the destruction to be *otherworldly* – "The *fire of God* fell from heaven and burned up the sheep and the servants…".[17] All of the destruction taken together was beyond comprehension. How could so much belonging to one person be destroyed in the course of a day?

And lest we say with our separation of time from the horrible events, "Well, it's just stuff," let us remember that *it represented far more than "just stuff."*

Amongst the animals destroyed were "many servants,"[18] and from what we know about Job's character, he was concerned and loving to all. The loss of those who worked for him and *with him* would have been *emotionally* devastating. Indeed, anyone would likely question how God could allow this to happen?

Further, the wealth that the animals represented were not just selfish possessions. Job supported his family, his community, and even strangers with his wealth. In the ongoing discussions about Job it becomes clear that Job was genuinely generous in helping others. Many in the community would suffer as a result of Job's losses. This wealth also constituted a future blessing for his children and security for his wife if he died before she did.

This first day's damages were crushing. When Satan is unleashed, everyone who sees it is horrified at the crushing devastation.

Job takes it hard. He tears his robe, shaves his head, and falls on the ground. Impressively though, *he does worship*. He makes a strong statement of truth and affirms his respect for God. "Naked I came from my mother's womb, and naked I shall return. The LORD gave, and the LORD has taken away; blessed be the name of the LORD."[19]

It is a beautiful and right thing to say, although within it there is at least a bit of blame. Satan actually did this in his fury and in his desire to win the bet. Job places responsibility squarely on his God. Theologically, this is partially acceptable – for the LORD did grant permission for the Adversary to wreak this havoc. Yet Job's initial response may be more telling of his view of God's nature than the theology above would indicate.

Also, in Job's accepting and worshipful response is another factor we must consider. Man has learned much over the years about how we as creatures respond when faced with an excess of sorrow and tragedy – we call it the grief response.

The first phase is called denial, and it is generally agreed to be a protective function to allow us to handle the initial responsibilities that occur when bad things happen. Losing one important person is often so emotionally crushing that without the protective functions of grief we would not be able to continue.

Our Creator made us in such a way that we process trauma gradually and in stages. We deny, we get angry, we get hopeless, and eventually we learn to deal with life as it is after the loss.

Job experiences the initial loss and deals with it in much the same way as many of us could – not fully able to conceive of what has happened he stays strong and *worships*. He goes to something familiar, and he engages a mental script he has probably thought through long before the events of this day. He tears his clothes and shaves his head in the sorrow that he does experience, but the full magnitude of the loss is not yet comprehended.

Nor will it be. Satan is never satisfied until he gets his way. He is not going to allow Job to catch his breath just yet.

Up to this point, Job could be called a spiritual superstar. The writer notes, "In all of this Job did not sin or charge God with wrong."[20]

The Second Attack – Getting Personal

Sometime after the first attack we find Satan again before The Almighty and once again God brings up Job, mentioning, "He still holds fast his integrity, although you incited me to destroy him without reason"[21]

Satan's response to that is dramatic; "Skin for skin! All that a man has he will give for his life. But stretch out your hand and touch his bone and his flesh and he will curse you to your face."[22] Satan is desperate, he wants to win the wager. He wants Job to be *his*, if only to prove his own power.

God accepts the second wager and clears Satan to attack Job's health.

Satan does not do anything halfway. Job finds himself covered in boils from his head to his toes. As mentioned earlier, this is the point at which Job's wife makes her "Curse God and die"[23] pronouncement.

Job rebukes her, and tells her she is speaking as "one of the foolish women would speak"[24] and that they should accept both good and bad from God. Theologically this is correct, but is there a storm brewing in Job's heart that will soon be evident to all?

For a *final time* in this epic story, the writer notes, *"In all this Job does not sin with his lips."*

Is it because things are about to go badly awry?

Internal Grief and Friends

Some of Job's friends show up, from a distance they see him sitting on the ash heap. He is not even recognizable:

They raised their voices and wept, and they tore their robes and sprinkled dust on their heads toward heaven."[25]

They sit with Job for seven days without speaking, because they could see that *"his suffering was very great.*[26]

I don't know how many of us have suffered greatly like Job. I have one friend who was involved in a very tragic automobile accident – his entire family was in the car. He was in the back seat with his wife and their youngest son, while his oldest son was driving. His only daughter was in the front passenger seat.

As they headed west on I-40 toward a wedding, something was happening in the eastbound lane. Traffic had gotten rather backed up due to some slow 18-wheelers, and one guy who was in a hurry finally had a chance to pass one of the offending trucks. With his young daughter beside him, he aggressively passed a big rig but as he swung in front of the truck he locked his rear bumper into the front bumper of the bigger truck. This caused the semi driver to lose control and careen into the grassy median. In the process of attempting to get the truck stopped, he went into the oncoming traffic and slammed into my friend's car.

My friend, sitting in the back street, only heard his daughter exclaim her brother's name, and then the impact. When it was all over, the wife, older son, and daughter had perished. My friend and his youngest son were hospitalized with life-threatening injuries.

I think of Job sometimes when I think about my friend Terry. As he sat in the hospital horribly marred by the accident and going through repeated surgeries, the physical pain magnified the mental anguish he experienced. Restricted to a hospital bed for weeks, having numerous weeping scars, and at the same time reliving the horrible accident and the loss – where does a person go from there?

My wife and I would visit the father and son in the hospital - it was very hard to do. Seeing them in such bad shape, and having no words of comfort made for times of awkward silence. Plus, there was the recognition of the great fear – *this could happen to any of us*. Tragedies such as this force us to deal with possibilities at some level that we would rather ignore.

Seeing Job's friends show up and sit on the ground for seven days took on a more tender meaning after my friend's accident. I saw how hard it was to be with someone when you want to help them in a specific way – *but know you cannot*. There were no words for my dear suffering friend or his lone surviving son.

There were no adequate words for Job in his time of darkness.

Seven Days of Silence

Job and his friends sit for seven long days without saying a word.

Seven days.

In some ways I wish it was possible to see Job's notes from those seven long days. What went through his mind as he grieved and tried to wrap his mind around what had happened? What words did he exchange with God during this time, and in what tone? Did Job cry uncontrollably, or was he stone-faced? Was he able to sleep? Did he have nightmares if he did sleep? What did his emotional pain feel like added on top of his physical problems?

The words that spill out once the seven days of quiet are over are very telling. Job has processed much during this time – and his friends have been stewing on a lot of ideas as well. The dialogue that ensues is going to be interesting – poetic, polemic, praiseworthy, insulting, and questioning.

As we move forward, let us unpack the words of Job to see whether or not Satan would win his wager.

Chapter 3

Curses

Toward the end of the second chapter the writer mentions that up until that point, "Job did not sin with his lips."[27] The writer then tells us about the three friends showing up and sitting in silence with Job for seven days.

One has to wonder what was going through Job's mind. What were the words that flowed through his mind during these dark days of incredible anguish?

Several years ago, an F5 category tornado destroyed my wife's hometown in Alabama. We went down to visit a couple of weeks afterwards, and an old friend of the family who was also a mail carrier for the Postal Service offered to show us the devastation. This sweet lady knew just about everyone in Hackleburg, Alabama, where she had grown up and my wife had lived until the seventh grade. As we drove along the path the tornado travelled she would say things such as, "That's the tree where they found Jimmy," or "That was the new house where Shellie and Larry lived, nothing left."

Her face seemed almost emotionless, but on a regular basis her tears would stream down in quantities I had never seen from *anyone* before. She made no sound of sobbing. She was silent. Her face looked numb. But the tears flowed onto her clothing. At one point she pointed to her tears and said, "I'm sorry, this just happens, I can't control it."

No apology was needed. My wife and I were unable to comprehend the evidence of destruction we were seeing – yet our silent crier had lived through it and lost much. Her present emotional state was *involuntary.*

Deep grief and trauma powerfully impact every part of who we are.

It makes one wonder what the three friends observed during the seven silent days. Were there times when Job appeared to be ready to say something, only to once again retreat within himself? Were there frequent tears, sobbing, or a look of rage?

The story doesn't say, it simply states:

After this Job opened his mouth and cursed the day of his birth.[28]

Searching for Cursing

It is an interesting reference for us that Job "cursed" the day of his birth. The original word means to "bless," and so it's usage here and in the discussions previously about cursing God is obviously euphemistic. The word *curse* in the English sense is more appropriate.

When Job curses the day of his birth, he wishes it had never happened. His present misery is so great that he wishes he had been stillborn.

In other words, Job proclaims that he would have been better off without a birthday. His being given life was not a good thing, rather, he would rather not have had the privilege. I think at this point his emotional state, much as our tornado tour guide, was completely understandable.

But Job is about to move beyond his musings on his birth.

As we move forward into Job's statements, we want to keep the wager Satan made in mind. Do Job's words about God reflect a desire that God not be in his life? Does he see God as a thorn rather than as a rose? Does he express doubt over the goodness or rightness of God?

Let us listen carefully to what Job has to say. We will look together at a number of statements and consider their nature – do they reflect honor and esteem for God, or does Job see his Maker as an undesirable liability?

Does Satan succeed in his mission?

Statements about God by Job

1. *Why is light given to him who is in misery, and life to the bitter in soul... whom God has hedged in?*[29]

This is from Job's first conversation with his friends. He is still cursing the day of his birth. This statement about God "hedging" him in is perhaps subtle but important. It is a picture of an oppressor pushing you into a corner. You are trapped. This indicates an act of malice. Job believes that his suffering was caused by God – he will share more details of this in a later discourse. But his friend Eliphaz will reply to this in such a way that it is confirmed that Job's belief even at this early point in the story is that the Lord has hedged him in *unfairly.* In Job's view, God has made a mistake. Eliphaz will shortly present a differing (though wrong) explanation for the hedging actions of God (Eliphaz agrees God caused this, but for a *just* reason).

In this statement Job believes God has caused this, and it is not just or deserved.

2. *For the arrows of the Almighty are in me; my spirit drinks their poison; the terrors of God are arrayed against me.*[30]

To paraphrase, "God has aimed at me with his poison arrows and scored a direct hit! God is harmful to me, intentionally!" The God he has so beautifully and faithfully served is serving up "terrors" against him!

Job is saying that God has succeeded in causing him pain, but he is in error in his actions.

3. *When I say, 'My bed will comfort me, my couch will ease my complaint,' then you [the Lord] scare me with dreams and terrify me with visions, so that I would choose strangling and death rather than my bones...leave me alone, for my days are but a breath...What is man, that you make so much of him...and test him every moment? How long will you not look away from me?*[31]

This is a long thought, it strikes me as a *rant*. In modern terms, isn't he saying that, "even when I try to get comfortable, you (God) intentionally terrify me! I would rather be dead than in your care?" I would be much better off if you would just leave me alone!" Understand this; he is very explicitly claiming that his life would be better off without God's involvement!

Curse, much?

4. *Though I am in the right, I cannot answer him [God]...If I summoned him and he answered me, I would not believe that he was listening to*

my voice. For he [God] crushes me with a tempest and multiplies my wounds without cause; he will not let me get my breath, but fills me with bitterness.[32]

Consider this one carefully. Job is sure that God is the one harming him (not Satan) *but* Job is equally sure that he himself is "in the right!"[33] Furthermore, he is fully confident that God would not listen to him, and he knows that God is doing these horrible things to him "without cause!"[34] Job is accusing God of being mistaken at the least, and *unjust* at the worst! The latter becomes more significant as Job's words continue, but to accuse the Almighty of being unjust is to deny one of his core attributes – and in fact constitutes *blasphemy!*

Accusing God of being in the wrong as The One of righteousness would seem to be cursing God. Accusing him of not listening even though He is in the wrong is turning the One True God of the Universe into something resembling typical pagan gods; little gods who demonstrate very human characteristics born of selfishness and weakness.

But if Job is saying that God is unjust, that *is blasphemy.*

5. *...He destroys both the blameless and the wicked...he mocks at the calamity of the innocent. The earth is given into the hand of the wicked; he covers the faces of its judges – if it is not he, who then is it?*[35]

Much as in the previous statement, Job is portraying the LORD as someone with an impetuous pagan nature. To paraphrase loosely, "He hurts everyone and then makes fun of their trouble! He directly causes the world to be taken over by evil people, and he blinds the judges so that only evil triumphs!"

It is no wonder that at the end of this particular discourse that Zophar explodes in anger! He shouts:

Should a multitude of words go unanswered, and a man full of talk be judged right? Should your babble silence men, and when you mock, shall no one shame you?[36]

Hearing Job make such accusations of apathy, arrogance, evil, and injustice was more than Zophar could stand. Much has been made of the unhelpful nature of Job's three friends in their words, and indeed God even makes much of it! But part of their response is fully justified! Isn't Job, by reducing God to an uncaring, unfair, and mocking pagan-ish god – cursing God?

Is it possible that Satan was just full of glee at this point? His plan was succeeding – Job had arrived at rock-bottom and grabbed his shovel and started digging. Certainly, God would soon kick this cursing and broken man to the curb. Satan's victory was looking more and more certain!

6. *If I say, 'I will forget my complaint, I will put off my sad face, and be of good cheer,' I become afraid of all my suffering, for I know you will not hold me innocent. I shall be condemned, why then do I labor in vain?*[37]

Job is contending that if he were just to buck up and put a smile on his dial that it wouldn't matter, that God would hold him guilty and continue to punish him even though *he [Job] is so righteou*s!

But here is the biggest point to consider; Job at this point in the midst of the wager considers his service to God to be "in vain!"[38] In other words, *every good thing I've even done for this God has been a waste of time!* This comes from out loud from a person who was terribly concerned earlier about one of his children just *thinking* an improper thought about the character of God *"in their hearts!"*[39]

Job shouts his curse to the heavens for all to hear – *serving God is a fool's errand!*

Truly cringeworthy.

7. *If I wash myself with snow and cleanse my hands with lye, yet you [God] will plunge me into a pit, and my own clothes will abhor me...There is no arbiter between us.*[40]

How does someone take this statement as a praise of God? How can this statement show respect and honor to the one toward whom it is directed? How is it not taken as a besmirching of the character and nature of God? He is saying, in effect, "No matter how righteous I try to be, he's still going to do me harm!"

But even more damning is the final statement from above – Job insinuates that he is unable to receive justice because there is no *arbiter* to mediate between God and himself! In other words, the only way he or anyone else could make God be fair or just is to have someone who could sit between us and *mediate* between us and God in order to force him to make a fair judgement! Is this not blasphemy? Who would be qualified to *make* the Almighty be fair?

8. *I will say to God, do not condemn me; let me know why you contend against me. Does it seem good to you to oppress, to despise the work of your hands and favor the designs of the wicked?*[41]

Job is saying that God *is oppressive*. He is fully ready to stand before God and lecture him by questions, i.e. "so why is it that you choose to do wrong to me?" God is *despising* his own work; this paints a very sociopathic view of God.

9. *...You seek out my iniquity and search for my sin, although you know that I am not guilty and there is none to deliver out of your hand...and you have destroyed me altogether. Remember that you have made me like clay...*[42]

Once again, Job's contention is that God is aggressively attacking him *even though God knows Job is completely innocent!* This is a charge against God that he is unjust, uncaring, and further demonstrates the presumption of Job; who seems to consider himself above reproach! He has no problem condemning the source of justice and righteousness while exonerating himself fully as being in the right.

Then there is the little *reminder* that Job presumes to give to God, in effect saying, "In case you are absent minded, I'm just a weak creature and you are all powerful, so go easy on me – you seem to have forgotten that!"

As mentioned before, Job is a man undergoing tremendous suffering, and these observations are not offered as a critique of the man – rather, we *are attempting to critique those who contend that Job did it right, that he is the hero of the book!* My goal is to perhaps give Job a chance to speak to us what he learned from the experience – I believe he would recommend a completely different hero to us!

10. *Are not my days few? Then cease, and leave me alone, that I may find a little cheer...*[43]

Once again, a recurring theme in these discourses is that Job's life would be better off without God in it. He is certain that God is being unjust and making his life horrendous. He is certain that he has no hope of recourse. Is Job cursing his Maker?

11. *Though he slay me, I will hope in him; yet I will argue my ways to his face.*

This will be my salvation, that the godless shall not come before him.[44]

I can still hear a certain preacher quoting *part of this verse* from more than a decade ago. He had a booming deep melodious tone, as he shared, "Though he slay me, I will hope in him!" Then he went on to state, "What a magnificent statement of faith in the face of suffering!"

But is it?

He didn't read the whole passage. One of the first rules in Bible interpretation is "never read a Bible verse"[45] This sounds funny, but after reading the larger quote above and then hearing the misuse of it from the pulpit you get the point! Sure, the initial words sound very strong and faithful, until you read what follows! You have to read more than just one verse!

"I will argue my ways to his face"[46] implies once again that God has made a grievous error in harming Job the way he obviously has. This reflects an interesting belief on Job's part that will be covered later, but it also once again brings up Job's core contention that in this case God is unjust, uncaring, and needs to be straightened out!

And who will straighten out the sovereign Lord of the universe? Why, just listen:

I will argue my ways to his face. This will be my salvation, that the godless shall not come before him.[47]

Job judges himself worthy of walking boldly before the throne of God and stating, in effect, "Hey, we need to talk – you've done me wrong and do not realize it, let me tell you why!"

Is this not an insult to the character and intelligence of God? Does this not constitute a curse?

12. *Surely now God has worn me out; he has made desolate all my company. And he has shriveled me up, which is a witness against me, and my leanness has risen up against me; it testifies to my face. He has torn me in his wrath and hated me; he has gnashed his teeth at me...he broke me apart; he seized me by the neck and dashed me to pieces; he set me up as his target; his archers surround me. He slashes open my kidneys and does not spare; he pours out my gall upon the ground. He breaks me with breach upon breach; he runs upon me like a warrior.*[48]

Not much comment needed in this phrase. As the discussions with the friends go on, Job is fully venting his pain and frustration with who he perceives to be a God in the wrong. This God is a curse to him, because of his grave error in the way he has dealt with one so righteous as Job considers himself to be.

13. *Behold I cry out, 'Violence!' but I am not answered; I call for help but there is no justice.*[49]

For those of you who are deep thinkers, this statement likely seals the deal. From a theological standpoint, this is the most damning statement of all against God and fully indicative of the truth that Job did indeed curse his Creator.

Our whole concept of *justice* as children of the living God stems from God himself. What is just, right, or fair in life is fully in reference to the character of God *alone*.

In looking at the Old Law, we find a large set of rules for daily life as well as some ceremonial rules. The detailed laws for daily life are very specific, dealing with issues such as theft, accidental death, homicide, sexual behavior, and other common problems that occur between people in society.

These rules were covenantal for Israel, but for us they are still vital in that they are not mere rules made by a man who wants to be in charge. You see, the rules of the Old Law flow from who God *is*. He created us as his creatures, and he wants the best for us. He wants to love us and for us to love each other. As our designer and Creator, he knows the purposes for which he made us, our weaknesses, and our needs. Thus, the rules contained in the Old Law are not just something he arbitrarily made up as some sort of a test; they are reflective of his heart and his all-knowing nature. The laws which God has given to man are reflective of who God is to the core of his being. They are the substance of his love for his creation.

And thus, when Job states "there is no justice,"[50] he is in effect either attacking the character of God or denying his existence as a pure and holy being. This statement is very close to Nietzsche's infamous "God is dead" proclamation.

While Job is certainly speaking from immense pain compounded by the frustration of his friend's insistence on his guilt of an unconfessed sin, this statement is crucial to our point.

Job cursed God.

Spokesman for Job

I've had this conversation with many when teaching this story. I share these very direct and understandable sayings of Job and someone will say, "But it is certainly understandable that he would feel this way!"

And indeed *it is* understandable. Our purpose is not to heap criticism on Job in his suffering. As mentioned before, I shudder to think of how I would handle a much lesser tragedy. Job's response was very *human.* In almost every aspect of what Job did, I cannot imagine myself or anyone I know handling it as well as Job did, yet it is clear that Satan succeeded in his goal of getting this man of God to curse the Almighty.

The purpose of this section of the book is to defuse some of the past misinterpretations of the story. The goal is, as best we can so far removed, to allow Job's voice to be heard again. *What would he share about this experience in which he was caught in a vicious battle between good and evil?*

For now, let us just allow Job to tell us to keep an open mind and *keep reading.* Going forward from Job's comments about there *being no justice,* he has three more discourses in which he defends himself against the contentions of his friends. He continues to accuse God of wrongdoing toward himself.

We must not miss the point however, that in spite of the *curses* Job never lets go of God. He is angry with him, believes God to be in error and owes him an explanation, but yet never releases his grip on his Lord. This is the *patience* or *steadfastness*[51] noted by the writer James in the New Testament.

In this dogged determination to stay with his God in spite of his perception of wrong-doing on his behalf we find perhaps another word of wisdom which Job might share with us; *in the midst of trials, never let go of the hand of God.* You may be angry, confused, hurt, and feel completely at a loss to understand anything that is going on around, but just as a child clings to their mother or father when scared, cling to your Father when you are in pain and confusion.

Because the Almighty, as we shall see, will not let go of you.

Did Satan Win His Prize?

Going back to the original scene before the Almighty. God brings up a certain man who is faithful and righteous. Satan knows this man very well, apparently Job has been a burr in his saddle for some time.

So, Satan makes his wager. Stop protecting him, take away the benefits of serving God, and he will naturally curse you to your face. And just as Job believed, just as Job's wife believed, and as we shall see, probably as Job's friends believed, Job would be cast away from the presence of God forever. This even seems to dovetail into the third of the Ten Commandments given to Israel:

You shall not take the name of the LORD your God in vain, for the LORD will not hold him guiltless who takes his name in vain.[52]

This is, after all, what is known as *blasphemy.* It would seem that Satan had won the bet. He had to be thrilled as he heard Job's accusations against God and his denial of the justice of the most holy God. Job's friends in their responses to these accusations were strong and full of warning.

Satan obtained the curses against the Almighty he desired.

Now what?

Job has cursed God. But Job has suffered so much.

God is going to speak to this small band of men. What will the God of grace and mercy say to Job?

CHAPTER 4

WITHOUT REASON?

It appears Satan won the bet – Job cursed his God.

Job, Satan, Job's wife, and Job's three friends all seem to share the conviction that if you say something bad about God, even just in your heart, then you are finished.

But what if there is something wonderful in this horrible test that God permitted? What if God agreed to this in part in order to teach us something about *himself?* The idea that *most* of the characters in the story agree to is that *cursing God,* saying something unfavorable about him, will lead to being rejected and damned. Does God want to make something clear to us about the true nature of his character through the trials of Job?

What if the lesson God intended to teach *from the beginning* of Satan's wager was something so wonderful that it could help us find peace in each day of our walk with the Almighty, no matter if the day was good or bad? What if our Creator wanted to demonstrate to each one of his beloved children a truth so precious that grasping it would give us a strength of faith we could never have imagined?

I believe that is what this story is really about. It isn't just about the *problem of suffering* as I was taught in earlier years – although it certainly teaches us something about suffering. It isn't about a man who was a spiritual superstar because he handled challenges in a way that made God happy. And God gives a really big *hint* about this early on in his conversation with Satan when he states:

He [Job] still holds fast his integrity, although you incited me against him without reason.[53]

Without Reason – What Did God Mean?

In the religious circles I run in, this has usually been interpreted to be a statement regarding the injustice against Job, because Job was righteous. As we have mentioned earlier, Job as a created being has definitely had some great moments. Thus this statement is seen as an explanation that Satan created an injustice by hurting someone who did not deserve to be hurt.

But when God shows up to speak to Job and his friends, what happens is so stunning and, shall we say, unexpected?

If God meant by *without reason* that it was unfair of Satan to oppress a *good man,* then we would expect God to respond to Job with gentleness and compassion.

But when we look at how God responds and *who* he responds to first – *his response is not at all reflective of gentleness and compassion!* If you are still not sure that Satan won in his efforts to get Job to curse God, *the response of the Almighty should remove all doubts!*

But in the end, we shall see the wonderous message that makes sense of God's mentioning that Satan's actions were *without reason.* And that message is life transforming!

Brace Yourself...

Let us imagine the scene that unfolds before us when God begins to address the miserable man Job and his friends as they sit on the ash heap.

One of those present in his discourse had been poetically describing what is happening around them just prior to the Almighty beginning his discourse. A great storm has been blowing up, with towering clouds, lightning, thunder, and wind. The storm moves closer to this huddle of men, centered around a man who has lost nearly everything, who is in the midst of intense emotional, physical, and spiritual pain. The wind, dust, rain, and sound pelt the poor man who is recently *childless* and whose future financial security has been wiped out. He is barely recognizable to those who knew him. He pathetically sits helpless as a massive storm adds insult to the injuries he has endured, that in his understanding were a result of God making a mistake in judgment.

A whirlwind drops down from one of the thunderclouds, and this band of friends watch in horror as it approaches. They are exposed and helpless – and then something more terrible happens.

A voice thunders from the whirlwind – *the voice of God himself.*

Will he deal with the harsh judgment of the friends of Job. Will he criticize Job's wife? Will he apologize and empathize with the unfair suffering Job has endured?

The first words thunder from this meteorological terror and pound one man square in the chest.

The words are brutal and very much directed at the heart and words of *that* man.

God speaks severely to *Job first!*

> *Who is this that questions my wisdom with such ignorant words? Brace*

yourself like a man, because I have some questions for you, and you must answer them.[54]

Wow! This is the God of mercy and grace?

Does it not seem harsh that the Almighty would direct such words towards someone who has just experienced the loss of *10 children,* his wealth, and his health? If we were to imagine ourselves being a speechwriter for God, might we suggest for public relations purposes that the Creator say something more along the lines of:

Hey Job, I am so sorry you had to go through all of this. This was horrible for you, and I know how you must feel. Satan was trying to prove something, so I had to let him go after you for a while – but you know I'm going to make everything better and you certainly didn't deserve this!

But no, God demands to know *who Job thinks he is* to ask questions of the omniscient One with very ignorant words! And if that were not enough, he tells this barely recognizable pathetically weak and suffering man to *brace himself,* or perhaps we could paraphrase this as "stop whining and sit up straight!"

For those who consider Job to be the hero of the book, God just made it clear that in *his judgment, Job is not in any way the hero!* The story of Job is not about Job at all. It is about something much greater and more beneficent than just an account of one man doing great and godly things through his own effort.

The ways of God are so far above the ways of man!

Job's Creator is about to launch into a series of questions that demonstrates the majesty, sovereignty and amazing nature of the Almighty. He is also going to, through his questions, confirm that Job did curse his maker and that such cursing is sin. It is indeed one of the most dreaded sins of the Bible called *blasphemy.*

More importantly, God will teach Job and those who loved him two wondrous and priceless faith lessons that day.

Ouch

Just as we looked at some of the key *curses* of Job and unpacked them, let us now look at some of the stronger words that God had for the poor man.

> 1.   *Where were you when I laid the foundation of the earth? Tell me, if you have understanding. Who determined its measurements — surely you know!*[55]

Job in his accusations against God repeatedly expressed his intent and desire to "argue my ways to his [God's] face."[56] Job even thinks so highly of his own intelligence, understanding, and righteousness that he *instructs God* of what *he* requires:

> *Then call, and I will answer, or let me speak, and you reply to me. How many are my iniquities and my sins? Make me know my transgression and my sin. Why do you hide your face and count me as your enemy?*[57]

God's question back to Job about his overall attitude and tone flattens Job immediately. It is as if the Creator reminds Job of what *is* – "Oh, so you are so amazingly wise and all-knowing, enough to demand an answer from God! So, where were you when *I created everything?*"

The next phrase seems sarcastic, but I believe it is instead *instructive* to each of us to remember our place – and more importantly, to remember *God's place in his universe.* "Who determined the measurements of the foundation of the earth, you're so brilliant that you must know," might be a proper paraphrase!

Using our imagination, and placing ourselves with this group of friends, can we sense the weight of the question? What if one of us had questioned the goodness and righteousness of the One who created all things and gave us life? What if in the stress of daily life one of us had cursed or blasphemed our Maker?

Do not these questions about the design and creation of the earth, along with the almost funny contrast of the limitations of human knowledge cause one to cringe? Could not God have simply made this one comment and have been done with the case?

Besides, speaking from out of the whirlwind would have been demonstration enough of his power and authority!

If we could be a spokesman for Job, given the hindsight provided by the author of the story, we might say the first lesson learned was:

- *God is God, and I'm not all that. Remember that it is okay to express our confusion and pain before God, but we must respect his all-knowing nature.*

2. *Will you discredit my justice and condemn me just to prove you are right?*[58]

As Job spoke from his pain and made his accusations against God's justice and for his own absolute righteousness, you sense a frustration in him that his Lord was not willing to listen. Here we find out, that the Almighty heard *every single word*. When I read the story I often put myself in Job's place and even read the words aloud. The words are full of accusation and condemnation toward the One who gave me life. This question to Job makes me cringe. And it makes me cringe because I can see myself saying similar things under far less stressful conditions.

But what makes me literally feel sick is to hear God repeat back the essence of what Job said in his suffering. As I've repeatedly said, I do not see myself being able to endure even a portion of what Job did as well as he did – so I *get* what Job is saying. It is understandable to feel this way toward God when it seems he has at the very least abandoned you!

But suddenly in this moment when Job experiences the absolute power and glory of God – what a terror it must have been to hear the loving and beautiful God of all creation repeat back the words and thoughts of your mouth *and* heart to you. I wonder if God ever did that for me from certain parts of my life if I wouldn't literally die of a massive heart attack – and in this is a great lesson.

Life is full of difficulties, but God is greater than all of our difficulties. But as he is unlimited and we are so limited, we must realize that there are times in life in which our limitations prevent us from seeing the *long view*. Our emotional and physical pain blind us to the incomplete and inadequate view of God that resides within our heart. It is natural in our weak state to lash out at our Creator – but would Job have something to say to us today? I consider that he might tell us:

- *The Lord of all creation is more wonderful, just, and holy than I ever realized. When we suffer, we should tell God that we are hurting and that we do not understand what is happening – but we do very well to not condemn God due to our lack of understanding.*

The Ferocious Storm

Greater than the winds, lightning, thunder and whirlwind are the words of God directed toward Job. This is an unreal and difficult scene to process as a created child of the Almighty. It was especially difficult for me given the way the book was taught to me as a child – that Job did it right and his friend were in the wrong.

Further, the theme of the book is supposedly about the *problem of suffering;* but on this barren plain with Job and these men of old gathered round, there is something much bigger afoot than just human suffering.

It is the problem of God himself.

It seems that Satan won the wager, at least in the terms of getting Job to curse God. God's words from the whirlwind are harsh and thunderous – indeed they seem capable of crushing the pathetic and broken man to whom they are addressed.

At this point our thoughts race – especially if it were our first time to read through it. *God* brought up Job with Satan and made him a target. Why would a loving God do that? Job seems to be one of the most excellent men to ever walk the face of the earth - why would God lay him out for abuse? When Job finally cracks under the strain, God speaks to him in severity. He asks him one unanswerable question after another and at times seems almost sarcastic in his words.

Further, if we imagine we have never read the story before and didn't know the end, will God do what Satan, Job, Job's wife, and the three friends pretty much expect him to do as a result of the cursing – will the God who set his loyal one up to be harmed by Satan cast him away forever?

Did Satan win this bet?

In our human weakness we continually try to mash God down into something more manageable and easier to comprehend – just as Job did. His friends did the same. We endow the eternal and Holy One with very human characteristics, and we expect him to do what *we* would do in our finite wisdom and understanding – and in this we make a grave error. We reduce the eternal Creator to something resembling the created being – weak and full of errors.

Is it possible that Satan made the same error? Did his wager reflect a view of God utterly beneath the majesty of the one whose throne he used to hover above?

Since Satan obtained the *curse* from Job he desired, did he win the wager?

And what did God mean when he stated that the whole bet was *without reason?*

Perhaps we should let Job answer that. And perhaps we will find something wonderful in God's plan that can strengthen our relationship with God in the process.

CHAPTER 5

TOO WONDERFUL?

All of us likely realize that life can kick us in the teeth with no warning. Even the best day has a bitter edge to it, because at the very least, it will come to an end.

The young bride so thrilled with her new husband may sense a nagging truth in the back of her head while still covered by her veil – this man someday could hurt me more than anyone else on earth.

Young first-time parents look into the bleary but beautiful eyes of their newborn child, and a sudden reality hits them – the child is fragile, delicate, and could be hurt or killed so easily. The potential of pain and loss is so great that most of us cannot think about this for too long.

All around us people are suffering – weekly and sometimes daily we hear of someone diagnosed with cancer, someone too-young dying of a heart-attack or in an accident. Horrible things happen to those we care about, and we struggle with God as we ask, "why?"

And in our pain, many of us even lash out at the one who gave us life. We utter curses under our breath, and we doubt that he is even there, because, well, there seems to be no justice. And yet we worry, does God hate me because I doubt and complain?

Further, we are not even sure if we can endure the potential hardships that loom darkly before us. How can we get up each day and find the joy that our Bibles tell us we *should* have in our walk with the Lord when there is so much pain and hardship facing each of us?

Back to the Storm

Satan is anxious – likely feeling he is about to be vindicated. He has a string of victories over the creatures God made and loves so much, but this one will be sweeter than most. This man Job, who was seemingly untouchable, has done exactly what Satan intended – he cursed the One who gave him life and every good thing.

And although Job has not abandoned God, which is remarkable in itself, Satan shares Job's belief that the cursing will make Job's faithfulness worthless; for *no one* can curse God and stay in his grace. He and the one he tortured were convinced of the finality of speaking ill of the Almighty.

So Job is about to speak – after all of the impossible questions and the harsh judgment, this one who has lost so much *because* he was serving God is about to share with us what he learned.

Job's words are breathtaking, especially considering all we have seen and heard up until this point. This man who has lost so much, who is in such bad shape physically and emotionally, and who is so ready to walk straight up to God and defend the innocence he knows he possesses – is suddenly *transformed into a different man altogether*. In this radical transformation over a matter of minutes is found the reason why the story of Job is about so much more than just the *problem of human suffering.*

In this rapid change of heart and character is found the key to living joyfully even when circumstances would seem to demand otherwise. In this metamorphosis of Job is found the spiritual secret of actually living out the words of Jesus when he said, "...do not be anxious about your life..."[59].

Do I have your interest? In spite of loss of 10 children, his beloved servants, his security found in the wealth he had wisely worked for, and his still pathetically poor health, Job ends up saying (in the modern tongue), "I'm good!"

Let's unpack Job's words and see what their transforming power was and is.

Learning from Job's First Response

We looked briefly at Job's first words to God earlier – but they are worth revisiting. They set the tone that helps us understand the secret to Job's transformation. Let' see if we can make sense of what he replied to God's first series of questions. Immediately before Job's first brief reply to God, the Almighty asks:

> *Do you still want to argue with the almighty? You are God's critic, but do you have the answers?[60]*

Job then answers:

> *I am nothing – how could I ever find the answers? I will cover my mouth with my hand. I have said too much already. I have nothing more to say.[61]*

Can you sense the realization of the greatness of God? This boil-covered man who was so ready to defend his righteousness and impose an inquisition on his Maker now covers his mouth. The defiant and self-righteous man who has lost so much now can only see one thing. He is completely humbled.

Do you get it? What was it that so quickly was able to get Job to forget his earlier conviction that God was in the wrong and unjust? Was it the questions, or was it something else? I would suggest that it was more than just the questions – but God then *continues* the questions.

What Job Now Knows

When God pauses after the second round of questions, Job speaks his final words of the story, and they tell us something we would all be so blessed to know. Let's attempt to look at the thoughts of Job and allow him to teach us what he learned from the voice from the whirlwind:

1. *I know that you can do all things, and that no purpose of yours can be thwarted.*[62]

In the few moments since God appeared, Job now understands something major. God has purpose. He *always* has purpose and intent. Whether or not we can comprehend it, God has something going on. Our inability to understand what God is doing is not sufficient cause for us to attack God or doubt him.

Perhaps what is more fascinating still, is that Job perceives a purpose of God in all of the horrible things that have happened to him. How could this be? Let us read on.

2. *'Who is this that hides counsel without knowledge?' Therefore I have uttered what I did not understand, things too wonderful for me, which I did not know.*[63]

Job restates God's question from earlier as the basis for *the most profound statement Job makes throughout his whole story.* Another version phrases the Almighty's words more breathtakingly; "Who is this that questions my wisdom with such ignorance?"[64] It seems that Job learned something lifechanging almost from the first moment God began asking questions. If each one of us could grasp the same, our lives would be changed forever.

For the suffering man, the one who lost all 10 of his children, his beloved servants, his wealth, and his health – now grasps within his broken heart something, well, *wonderful!*

There is something new in his life and heart that makes the unimaginable grief of Satan's attack dissipate – what Job comprehends is so much greater than any earthly concern that it envelopes Job's world and makes everything else insignificant.

Or perhaps I should not say "what" it is that now covers Job, but rather "who."

Job has experienced the presence, the glory, the power, the person, the magnitude, the wisdom, the constancy, and the absolute otherworldliness of *God Himself, in person.*

In that whirlwind, when the first sound of the voice of the Creator emerged, Job's confident conviction of his own righteousness was obliterated by the absolute purity and power of the presence of the One in whose image he had been made.

The painful images of the faces of his children, servants, and everything else he had lost *could not remain while Yahweh was present.*

Moses had experienced this, indeed had requested this transforming presence. He had pleaded with his Maker, "Please, show me your glory."[65]

God's answer to his friend lets us know some of the why behind Job's statement about things being "too wonderful"[66] for him:

> *"I will make all my goodness pass before you…but…you cannot see my face, for*
> *man shall not see me and live."[67]*

This boggles the mind, how could experiencing God create such an emotional/ physical disturbance that it could, well, kill you?

It is instructive that as Moses' experience goes, that the Almighty takes great measures to protect Moses, yet *he wants Moses to* have *this amazing* experience:

> *"Behold, there is a place by me where you shall stand on the rock, and while*
> *my glory passes by I will put you in a cleft of the rock, and I will cover you with my*
> *hand until I have passed by. Then I will take away my hand, and you shall see my*
> *back, but my face shall not be seen."[68]*

Do you get it? At some point in Moses' and Job's life, God wanted this child of faith to experience his glory in a larger measure. Why?

That takes us to the next words of Job.

> 3.   *'Hear, and I will speak; I will question you, and you make it*
> *known to me.' I had heard of you by the hearing of the ear, but now my*
> *eye sees you; therefore I despise myself, and repent in dust and ashes.[69]*

If Job could sit down with us and share what he learned, which is what this book is really about, I believe this would be one of the two main points he would grab us by the shoulders and *shout at us*. Job knew a lot *about* God, and *he tried to serve him as best he could given what he knew.* But in his encounter with the God who spoke to him from a whirlwind, Job discovered something *amazing.*

The God whose *presence enveloped and overwhelmed him in the whirlwind was completely captivating compared to the smaller version of God he had served earlier.* It wasn't that Job was following a false God, it was just that his view of God was entirely inadequate and beneath the majesty of the One True God. In this whirlwind experience, Job's relationship took an exponential leap of knowledge – from knowing *about* God to *experiencing the reality of who God is!*

As Job sat there in the whirlwind, his old view of God was shattered. His high view of his own self, also, was utterly destroyed.

Job was a good man, as created beings go. But he was no hero. Bathed in the glory of God, he was stripped naked of any idea of God owing him anything for his previous good behavior. The very notion of God listening to him lecture about the *mistakes* God had made in bringing on his suffering now made him want to vomit. He had spoken rashly from his pain, and now he truly *despised* himself for doing so.

The glory of God. As anyone seeks to know him initially, there is no possible way to become instantly aware of the glory of God. As God pointed out to Moses, to suddenly experience all that God is would literally overwhelm and result in our death. The Almighty is so wondrous and his power emanates from his core being to such an amazing extent that we could not handle it all at once.

Yet the Creator of us all *wants us to experience his presence, his glory, his love, his power, and his otherworldliness as we are able!* To experience even a portion of what Job did will transform our hearts and our walk to something that will amaze the world.

Repentance

I despise myself, and repent in dust and ashes.[70]

This is a man convicted by God's word of his blasphemous heart. Job is not the hero, he is the sinner. Those are his words, not mine. He held fast to God patiently, but *he sinned in magnifying himself and presuming he could stand before God and tell him of his many mistakes.*

Job accused God of being his adversary, of making his life miserable. He lamented to his friends that he desired that his Maker would leave him alone so he could enjoy life. He repeatedly expressed his confidence that he would lecture God on what he had done wrong in dealing with him during those disastrous two days of Satan's fury. He suggested that God enabled the wicked to flourish, and that there was no value in following God. He denied that justice was an immutable trait of the Almighty.

Then there was the premise that started all of this. It was the conviction of Satan, Job, Job's wife, and of Job's friends. It was the strongly held belief that God is great, but if you get on his bad side, if you accidently curse him in your heart, or if you have secret sin in your life – God will strike you with suffering, death, and banish you from his presence. For that matter, Job's friend Bildad even suggested that the death of Job's ten children was the direct result of their sinning against God![71] What a monstrous portrayal of the Creator!

When Job, however, is surrounded by the very amazing and powerful presence of the one true living God of all Creation – he fully understands just how badly he had blasphemed who God truly is. And so, he repents in dust and ashes. The glory of God has bared his soul and shown him that he was dead wrong to declare God to be in the wrong. He was grievously in error to curse his Maker.

Satan got what he wanted.

Or did he?

We will get the final verdict from the Creator of all things in the next chapter – but let's see what lessons we can learn from Job to grow in our relationship with God from these final words.

Lesson One – Knowing God is different from knowing about God.

I had only heard about you before, but now I have seen you with my own eyes.[72]

Job's *service* to God up to the point of the trial Satan imposed had been amazing. After *experiencing God, Job's God was amazing!* Job, before the tragic events of this story, had done so much, given so much, and helped so many in the pursuit of serving and pleasing God. That was good and right.

But now, he sits stunned that God *is so pleasing*, and does such good, and helps so many. The sensory experience of being immersed in the power and majesty of the Eternal Father has led Job to a *wonderful* conclusion: The Almighty is fully *wonder-full.* All of his losses now lie hidden behind the reality and beauty of who God is, every day.

God. Is. That. Great.

And so for us, how do we experience God in such a transforming way, that brings us to a true sense of awe in his presence?

First, we can do what we have just done – we *dwell* in the Word of God. We sit before God daily and ask the Holy Spirit to guide us as we read and meditate on stories such as Job, Mary, David, Paul, or Isaiah. We see Job's response after all that he lost, in saying that what he experienced was *too wonderful,* and we plead with God to make that real in our own hearts.

Does not the reality of the beauty of God that Job experienced make your heart burn within you? Have tears come to your eyes as you realize the true message of the story of Job?

Second, we can ask God to continue to show us more of his glory. As we saw with Job, God does listen to us.

He. Hears. Every. Word.

If we sincerely ask God to show us his glory in a measure that we can endure, will he not do it?

He may answer us by powerfully illuminating a Bible story such as Job. Or he might show us through nature, through the amazing and beautiful irreducible complexity of life. He might teach us through others. Or, he might show us more of who he is in a dream?

It was early 1989 when my view of who God was changed forever. I was raised in a very legalistic tradition, although we saw ourselves as just being *right* and probably the *only* true believers. But I, as a young man, found I could not keep all of the legal requirements perfectly and so I gave up – I became an evolution-believing atheistic naturalist.

After a few years, God chased me down and through a series of amazing events, he humbled me and brought me back. It was a prodigal son moment of sorts, except that I refused to wear the father's coat - I still (in keeping with my legalistic tradition) wanted to raise my own sheep and weave my own cotton. I was trying extremely hard to be right before God. I was determined *this time around* that I would be pleasing to God. I would be his hero!

One evening while I was in pilot training for the Air Force, I was waiting for my wife to come home from her job at the hospital. It had been a long week, and I was so tired I felt like I was bleeding from my eyes. I sat on the end of the bed with my feet on the floor, and eventually laid back on my back from that position. I fell asleep very quickly, and dreamed the shortest, most terrifying, most lifechanging, and most wonderful dream of my life.

In my dream, I was watching myself sleeping on the bed, as if I were standing at the end of the bed. Suddenly in the windows behind the bed, the brightest light I had ever seen broke through the night sky, and suddenly I was back in my body within my dream. But more impressive than the light, was the sense of the presence of someone with power and purity beyond any ability of comprehension. In my dream, my arms involuntarily raised above my head in a position of absolute praise, and I sat immediately up in bed, almost as if a giant hand lifted me. I was all at once terrified, in awe, and full of wonder at what was happening. Just as quickly, I awoke, sitting straight up with my hands over my head in the same position of praise they had been in my dream!

I quickly jumped completely onto the bed toward the windows in one movement. My hands grabbed the window frame and I stared with wide eyes toward the dark Arizona skies. My heart was racing faster than I had ever felt it beat, and tears flowed from my eyes involuntarily.

I was completely undone. It was a dream of the return of the LORD. There was nothing intellectual in this experience of the return, just an overwhelming experience of the incredible and indescribable glory of who the One True God of the universe is.

I quickly fell face first on the bed in worship, and began speaking to God more honestly than I ever had. I don't know the exact words, but it was something along the lines of, "I am so sorry, *I had no idea who you are*. I have been so wrong. I have been such a disgrace to your name." For nearly three decades I have sat and remembered the experience of that dream, and I am so thankful for it.

> *I had heard of you by the hearing of the ear, but now my eyes see you,*
> *therefore I despise myself, and repent in dust and ashes.*[73]

I give God the credit for the dream because it revealed something to me that I had never even remotely conceived of up to that point. I was in the Word regularly, preaching at our congregation in Arizona, teaching class, and doing good things. I knew about God, and I wanted to please him.

But that dream marked the point in my life when I began grappling with my idolatrous view of God. I had endowed him with petty human characteristics, and insulted him by thinking that I could bring something to the relationship that he would be so impressed with that he would be forced to love me. I had lived in fear of dying at the wrong time, when I wasn't being strong, or perhaps *cursed God* or poorly represented him, and then he would condemn me to hell.

I think my beliefs about God are the reason my fascination with this story has continued for so long now.

When I would in my mind's eye sit and watch Job lose so much, and then after his encounter with God talk about *wonderful things,* I sensed a certain kinship. I am a weak and broken man. I have no claim to fame based upon great deeds such as Job did prior to his whirlwind experience of God. But the wonder of *who God is to the core of his being has the ability to change us forever!*

But I sense God loved Job and myself so much that he showed us a measure of his glory – and we were both forever changed in our relationship with God.

Since that time my Creator has shown me more of his glory. It has occurred through devoted times of time in the Word, prayer, through nature, through events, and this his action in my life. The love of my wife, children, family and very precious friends have shown me the face of my loving Lord in increasing measure.

Ask God that he would increasingly show you his glory. Trust him to choose the method of revelation. When we begin to see even the *back* of God (as Moses did), when we perceive the power and majesty of God, our earthly problems begin to fade in importance.

The words of A.W. Tozer are so relevant here:

> *...The gravest question before the Church is always God Himself, and the most portentous fact about any man is not what he at a given time may say or do, but what he in his deep heart conceives God to be like. We tend by a secret law of the soul to move toward our mental image of God. This is true not only of the individual Christian, but of the company of Christians that composes the church... It is my opinion that the Christian conception of God current in these middle years of the twentieth century is so decadent as to be utterly beneath the dignity of the Most High God and actually to constitute for professed believers something amounting to a moral calamity.*[74]

If we believe that God the Father is, as Job and others did, punitive and easily susceptible to angrily casting us away if we happen to say something bad about him in our heart or do not meet certain performance standards – how will that affect our daily walk with him? Will we not be fearful of him, though his Word says:

> *There is no fear in love, but perfect love casts out fear. For fear has to do with punishment, and whoever fears has not been perfected in love."*[75]

Job seemed nervous about his adult children accidentally cursing God in their hearts while they were enjoying each other's company – he was fearful of a less than perfect love! He was a performing machine, he helped travelers, widows, the poor – he worked *so hard*. When trials came he strongly defended his own perceived perfect righteousness to the point of accusing God of having made a mistake.

But then, he encountered something "too wonderful"[76] that just didn't match up with his earlier conceptions of God. He admitted he "was talking about things I knew nothing about"[77] in his accusations of his Maker as being unjust.

The point is this: When Job was *bathed* in the glory of God, his whole understanding of the Lord changed. Not just his view of God, but *his view of the world*. The intensity and absolute purity and power of the living God pushed away all of his sufferings – and those were immeasurable. Job perceived God, in that moment on the burn pile, in such a way that in that moment with God clearly in view, *the glory of God was all that he could see.*

It was a vision of heaven. All tears, except tears of joy and amazement, were wiped away. In the warmth and love of the presence of God, Job understood at a heart level that everything was okay, because the Lord was his portion.

The Lord God Almighty was all Job had in that moment, and that was more than enough.

The takeaway from this first lesson is this. Seek to increasingly *know* God. Knowing about God is a natural first step, but prayerfully seek to increasingly be shown the glorious God of All in increasing measure. Dwell in the Word, be constant in prayer, keep your eyes and heart open – and ask God to show you his glory.

Your life will never be the same when you begin to see God as he is.

Lesson Two – When We Suffer, Remember that God Has a Purpose Greater than We Might Imagine

What possible purpose could all of Job's suffering have? Does God truly work all things together for good?[78] Well, Job perceived in his encounter with the God in the whirlwind that "no purpose of yours can be thwarted."[79] What was that purpose though? Remembering that God himself had expressed to Satan that the whole incitement of evil against Job was *without reason,* why did God permit it? *What was his purpose?*

Was it not to teach Job, a beloved child of God who was trying so hard, what the Almighty was truly like? Was it to show Job that he could watch his children enjoying themselves and not worry about when the other shoe would drop if one of them secretly just thought something bad about God? Was it not to show Job that he didn't have to wear himself out doing great things to be of immeasurable value to the Father? Was not this whole horrible experience allowed to take Job to the next level of understanding and faith when he would understand that *perfect love does truly cast out fear, and our Father is perfect?*

Job still had some grieving to do in the days after the whirlwind receded.[80] But wouldn't it stand to reason that as the grief receded, Job's joy in the Lord Himself was greater than ever. Would not his inner concept of God, as Tozer so well put it, have been so wonderful and loving that he awoke each morning relaxed and content to be in the unbreakable grip of grace of the Eternal Father? The pressure to perform was *gone*. The fear of an accidental slander against God and the resultant condemnation was *gone*. God's purpose in agreeing with Satan's wager was to show to a godly high achiever that having God as your Father was *all the achievement you needed.*

God's purpose enabled Job, and everyone who takes the time to struggle with the tortuous story, to realize that the pressure of pleasing a demanding and vengeful God is *over* for those who are his. No pressure, just joy. Hard times will come, but if *Job's* God is for us, who on earth or in heaven could ever do us harm?

We may not perceive God's purpose in this lifetime. But Job gently encourages us to trust that God always has a purpose, and we would do well to give our loving Father the benefit of the doubt.

CHAPTER 6

VERDICT

But stretch out your hand and touch his bone and his flesh and he will curse you to your face.[81]

Satan was right. Although Job was a very righteous man, the unreal losses he sustained at the hand of the Adversary were too much. Job cursed God.

So, Satan won the bet?

Not so quick.

Let us look one more time at God's response, keeping in mind that the Almighty had indeed said earlier that this whole wager was *without reason.* Did this caveat which God expressed from early on in the wager let us know that the Adversary's desires where doomed from the start?

God speaks to Job from the whirlwind. The words are harsh.

Who is this that darkens counsel with words without knowledge?[82]

> *Brace yourself like a man, because I have some questions for you, and you must answer them.*[83]

> *Where were you when I laid the foundations of the earth? Tell me if you know so much...What supports its foundations, and who laid its cornerstone as the*

morning stars sang together and all the angels shouted for joy?[84]

> *But of course, you know all this! For you [Job] were born before it was all created, and you are so very experienced!*[85]

Shall a faultfinder contend with the Almighty?[86]

> *Will you even put me in the wrong? Will you condemn me that you may be in the right? Have you an arm like God, and can you thunder with a voice like his?*[87]

Just reading the directness and boldness of God's words, Satan likely suspected that the wager was a win-win. The Deceiver had managed to obtain curses against God from Job's mouth; the first win. And the second win was coming. Surely in all of this invective directed toward this shell of a man was coming the pronouncement that Job and everyone suspected:

Behold, because of your blasphemy you are cast away from me forever!

Satan's joy is harm, destruction, and deceit. At the end of this seeming tirade of the Creator against his pathetic creature, Satan's joy was nearly complete. He eagerly awaited the pronouncement of Job's eternal doom.

The pronouncement *never comes*.

Without Reason

The words of the Almighty come rushing back from the very start of the story:

*Have you considered my servant Job, that there is none like him on earth, a blameless and upright man, who fears God and turns away from evil? He still holds fast his integrity, although you incited me to destroy him **without reason**.*[88]

God deals with the sin in Job's heart in his words from the whirlwind. Job repents, and states that he really didn't know how great and purposeful God truly was – but now he knows the *wonder* of the amazing and all-powerful God of the universe.

And so the disappointing (to Satan) pronouncement comes, not to Job, but to Eliphaz, Bildad, and Zophar:

> *My anger burns against you and against your two friends, for you have not spoken of me what is right, as my servant Job has. Now therefore take seven bulls and seven rams and go to my servant Job and offer up a burnt offering for yourselves. And my servant Job shall pray for you, for I will accept his prayer not to deal with you according to your folly. For you have not spoken of me what is right, as my servant Job has.*[89]

If we could be so bold as to presume to speak for the Adversary at that moment, might he say:

> *Wait, what? Job spoke what was right? He said you had no justice in any bone in your body! He said if you would leave him alone his life would be better! He said you crushed him and were badly mistaken in your treatment of him! You mean this is over! This is outrageous!*

And so, God's words are outrageous. It is outrageous grace, mercy, and love. It is an amazing demonstration of the tender compassion of the Almighty toward his creatures.

In other words, it is just another day in the heart of God.

You see, the reason (I perceive) Job's Creator stated that all of this horrible treatment of God was *without reason* is because the Father knew he would never let go of his child.

Job was his. He knew Job's heart, and he knew he would not ever let go of his Father. He knew that under sufficient emotional and spiritual strain that his human weakness would indeed cause him to lash out at his Creator, simply because to Job, his God ran the whole show. It was the only recourse Job knew. He had to yell at someone, and the Almighty God was the only one with enough power to cause such destruction.

God knew Satan had lost the wager the moment it was proposed. There was no reason to doubt the faithfulness of God toward one of his beloved children.

The wager brings to mind Psalm 2, a portion of which states:

> *Why do the nations rage and the peoples plot in vain? The kings of the earth set themselves and the rulers take counsel together against the LORD and against his Anointed, saying, 'Let us burst their bonds apart and cast away their cords from us.' He who sits in the heavens laughs; the Lord holds them in derision.*[90]

It is natural to look at some of the evil in the world, plotted and executed by mortal men and women under the influence of Satan and become very distressed. Is God distressed? According to the Psalm above, the Lord in heaven looks upon their feeble-minded schemes and *laughs.* The power of man does not keep the Lord up at night. *Neither does the scheming of Satan.*

Satan's power is limited; he is a defeated foe.

Satan, as a *created being*, proposed a wager to win Job from the hand of God, based upon the premise that a curse from Job to the face of God would be sufficient for God to condemn Job to an eternity of punishment. Satan believed the Almighty to be a short-tempered tyrant incapable of taking a verbal hit.

God laughed.

Who in heaven or on earth supposes that they can pry a beloved child of God from his hand? What monumental arrogance! What slander against the attributes of God!

Anytime God's creatures suffer, our Creator suffers alongside. He cares for his children, and is infuriated when harm is done against them.

But God is not impressed by the idiotic sociopathic evil that man, or Satan, creates in their hearts. He does not wring his hands and wonder, "Oh my, I really liked Job, I hope Satan doesn't force me to condemn him!"

God's loving hand *will not be forced by any created being!*

Job learned all of this and more when God's presence enveloped him on that ash heap. In spite of all of the *wrong* things Job said, he was solidly in the grip of God's amazing grace. Satan is a formidable and sadistic foe, but he is no match for the loving God who created each one of us because of his great love.

If you are God's child right now, you may be having trouble breathing. As you take in the majestic compassion and love your Father has for you and the love in your heart is directed toward him, you may feel the squeeze of the Almighty's powerful arms around you.

You are his. Period.

Job Spoke Right?

We focused on some of the less-than-worthy things Job said during his trial, making this statement of Job speaking what was right seem a bit odd. He *did* curse his Maker!

But one point needs to be made to pound home the grace, mercy, and absolute goodness of our loving Father.

At the very last, Job says that he knows that God has purpose, and that purpose will not be undone by man or any created being. He also confesses that he spoke of things that he had no clue about. And then he acknowledges that once he experienced the God he had cursed, he repented for his cursing.

And God said to Job, *you have spoken what is right!*

If you are pretty good at making things happen in life, as Job was, you may be thinking, "But Job said so many bad things! How can he get away with that?

That's human thinking. When we are good at performing we tend to *expect* that people will pay for poor performance. But then when a high-performer, or shall we say, a *self-righteous* person, really blows it – they suddenly see the value in *mercy and grace for themselves!*

Job was *righteous in his own eyes*[91] and yet his eyes were opened to true righteousness when he perceived the utterly perfect *holiness* of God. Perhaps he could have written the praise quite easily that day found elsewhere in the Word:

> *The LORD is merciful and gracious,*
>
> *slow to anger and abounding in steadfast love.*
>
> *He will not always chide,*
>
> *nor will he keep his anger forever.*
>
> *He does not deal with us according to our sins,*

nor repay us according to our iniquities.

For as high as the heavens are above the earth,

so great is his steadfast love toward those who fear him;

as far as the east is from the west,

so far does he remove our transgressions from us.

As a father shows compassion to his children,

so the LORD shows compassion to those who fear him.

For he knows our frame;

he remembers that we are dust.[92]

As far as the east is from the west! Ours sins are removed by God as far as they can be removed. Infinitely far, forgotten, and no longer there!

Satan lost the wager, *because of Who God is*. Job spoke what was right, because in the moment of repentance – in that moment when Job confessed that he spoke of what he did not at all understand, God *wiped the slate of wrong completely and utterly clean!*

As the psalmist above so beautifully stated, *Job's Father remembered that Job was made from dust, and he had loving compassion on him.* All of Job's harsh words spoken from his pain and confusion were now separated from him, *infinitely separated as far as the east is from the west.* Lest we forget, the east and the west *never* come together.

In the moment of repentance, of turning away from wrong things, Job was made right in the heart of his Creator. Job experienced in the presence of God "things too wonderful."[93]

The God of the Old Testament

There has been a contention made at times that there is such a thing as *the God of the Old Testament* who was very different in character than the one we see with the advent of Jesus the Messiah.

The story of Job shows this idea to be a gross misunderstanding and misrepresentation.

Satan's wager served only to demonstrate that this view of God having been different in earlier times is a fallacy.

And the LORD blessed the latter days of Job more than the beginning...[94]

Job of the Old Testament experienced what John the Apostle knew as "grace upon grace." [95] In spite of what Eliphaz, Bildad, and Zophar believed – Job was not suffering because of some unrepented sin on Job's part. In spite of what Satan, Job, and Job's wife believed – even cursing the One who created all things does not bring on eternal punishment. God does indeed remember, as the psalmists wrote, that we are creatures of dust. Job's God was full of compassion, grace, and mercy.

The vital takeaway from this whole terrible and wonderful story is the same as that delivered by the prophet Malachi. This messenger of God worked in a time when God's people had once again strayed far from the light of righteousness – and a judgment was coming. But along with the judgment was also a reminder:

For I the LORD do not change; therefore you, O children of Jacob, are not consumed.[96]

There are times when our evil becomes such an odious affront to Who God Is that he must act – and his actions are justly wrathful. But then also within the character of God is his mercy and grace – and therefore we *are not consumed!*

God is so kind-hearted and gracious. He always has been, and always will be. He can be no other way. This is *who he is.*

King David of the Old Testament knew intimately of the love and mercy of God. In one of his less-than-stellar moments, David had sinned before God and was offered a choice of discipline. The first option would be three-years of famine in his country. Or he could face three months of being pursued by his enemies. The final choice would be three-days of severe disease among his people, directed by the hand of God.

I've shared this with teens who were struggling in their concept of God, who saw him as arbitrary and harsh. I ask them whether David would choose famine, the limited power of man, or the unlimited power of God. Every one of them so far has answered the same – they believed the safest course was being pursued by man. They said this because man has limited power, and God has unlimited power. We all like to eat and drink, no one wants famine.

But then I share David's words, they are a praise of the *God of the Old Testament* that rings across the centuries:

> *I am in great distress. Let us fall into the hand of the LORD, for his mercy is great; but let me not fall into the hands of man.*[97]

David had spent a lot of time in the presence of the Almighty since his youth. He knew God, that his wrath *could* be formidable. But the wrath of his Lord was also always *justified.* In the long run, however, he knew God for one attribute above all else – *mercy.*

He also knew man very well. He had been hotly pursued by the crazy King Saul whom he was so loyal to, had his best friend Jonathan killed in battle, and had one of his own sons lead a coup that deposed him from his throne as King.

And of course, there was the Bathsheba-Uriah incident. He knew very *personally* the evil that man was capable of. He knew that even within his own heart, man's evil was *unjust and unlimited.* Just a note here, when man goes to the evil side we become just like the father of evil who executed all ten of Job's children in one gust of wind. We are capable of immense cruelty without remorse – we become sociopathic and selfish.

It is true as the psalmist proclaimed that *"the fear of the LORD is the beginning of wisdom."*[98] But each of us needs to move past the *beginning* of wisdom and grow into maturity. Beginning in the Word we must let God teach us Who He Is *in all of His beauty*, so that we too will learn as David did that it is better to trust God's discipline than man's evil heart.

The key thing about David is this. He knew the extreme grace and tender mercy better than most. In the earlier mentioned Bathsheba-Uriah incident, he well remembered the score. David knew that as an adulterer, liar, and *murderer* – that if only justice and wrath reigned in God's heart, he would have been *dead.*

David knew the *God of the Old Testament* as a Father who had a heart of tender love and compassion toward his children. He trusted God to always do what was right and just in his life.

Certainly at times God's people (and those who are in utter rebellion to him) have found themselves under judgment and facing severe penalties, including death. But when it comes to a child of God such as Job, punishment is not part of the picture. The writer of Hebrews makes it clear:

It is for discipline that you have to endure. God is treating you as sons. For what son is there whom his father does not discipline? I you are left without discipline, in which you all have participated, then you are illegitimate children and not sons.[99]

We noted earlier that far from being punishment, Job was caught up in the battle between God and Satan. Much of his suffering was *because* he was on God's side!

The God of the Old Testament is the same as the God of the New Testament and is the same as the God of the Universe today!

It is great news for all of us – if you are God's child just as Job was, you have nothing to fear. God will not let you go just because you crack under the pressure of life on earth. God has always and only been the amazing, compassionate, powerful, loving, merciful, caring, wise, and holy God he has always been.

And the verdict of Satan's wager is clear – the Judge ruled in favor of *himself.*

This attack on Job was in reality an attack on God himself. It was a portrayal of the character of God as being a short-tempered tyrant who could not take a verbal hit. It was the portrayal of the Almighty as a gleeful rule-maker just waiting for someone to violate a rule so he could condemn them.

God thunders from the bench, *"How about no?"*

Satan lost, and The Almighty won – as he always does. Job, his wife, and his friends won.

We won.

We *win!*

God wins, the odds are permanently stacked in his favor.

If there was ever any doubt, the hero of the story of Job is the Almighty God of Creation. I'm confident Job would agree.

CHAPTER 7

UNPACKING

What can we learn from the wager to strengthen our walk with God every day? Whether in good times or bad, the story of Job teaches us truths that can benefit us and glorify God every single day of our life. Let's unpack this amazing interaction between God, Satan, Job, and his closest friends and see what faith-building lessons are there for us:

1.   **God does have a plan – always.**

We see this in the wager, and in the two different horrible attacks of Satan. Even if the wager itself and Job's resulting suffering was *without reason, God still had his reasons! He had a plan!*

First of all, God demonstrated that Satan and Job's idea about God's children walking a thin line with their Creator was completely and utterly *false!* Job cursed God prolifically, and at the end of the day, Job was still in the loving arms of his heavenly Father! Satan could not shake Job loose from the caring embrace of his God. *Satan is not that powerful. God is ultimately powerful.*

Further, God made sure that someone *wrote down the account and that it was preserved until now!* He wants us to know who he was and is, and that we can trust him even when things look hopeless. He wants us to know that he loves us and that no one can shake us loose from his embrace.

But perhaps there was another reason God agreed to the wager, and even to the terrible losses Job would endure?

Reading about Job's righteousness as it is discussed throughout the story gives me a distinct impression that Job was very serious and zealous in his walk with God. As the story begins, God's words confirm that Job was a man of remarkable faith. As the Almighty puts it, "...there is *none like him on earth.*"[100] How many of us dream of the possibility of having a faith so remarkable that our Creator would bring it up from his throne? Can you imagine *your* name echoing in the halls of heaven, in the voice of the Father himself? *"Have you considered Jennifer? There is no one like her on earth?"* God's confidence in and knowledge of Job indicate that this believer was walking hard after God.

Job had reached a high level of maturity and spiritual discipline. In the words of some of the saints of old, he had devoted much effort in the area of *spiritual formation*.

God was pleased.

But how would God go about taking Job to a level he probably truly longed to attain? How would Job grow from the commendable faith he possessed to an even greater one?

In spite of Job's excellent faith, there was still room for growth. As the story notes, Job and others around him still held some views of God that were not quite right. Did this great man need to suffer the loss of nearly everything and deal with a world in which all that he had was God? Did Job need to reach a broken and impoverished state and experience a spiritual failure before he was ready to fully appreciate being bathed in the all-sufficient glory of God?

In other words, *did God go along with Satan's wager in order to allow Job to see the God he loved in a more beautiful and powerful way than he ever had?*

I am not assuming to sit on the throne and determine God's motives, but I am reflecting on the other stories of God as he interacted with people that he loved.

Moses experienced a massive failure in Egypt when he thought *his moment* to save his people had arrived. He murdered an Egyptian, had to flee to a remote area, and spent 40 years learning humility and the ways of the desert. It would seem the training with smelly sheep and the resultant humility Moses received was *necessary* for the good of Moses and the plan of God.

Joseph is mistreated by his brothers, Potiphar's wife, fellow inmates, and endures years of separation from his beloved father. His is an amazing story of enduring through years of hard-to-comprehend seeming abandonment by everyone *including God*. But God had a plan in Joseph's suffering, a plan which Joseph eventually embraced. Joseph saves his family and at least two nations – and understands that God had a plan in his suffering.

Esther had every reason to believe that God didn't care for her at all. Both parents had died, she was raised by an uncle, and then was taken from his home involuntarily to be put into a pagan king's harem – but it was all part of God's plan to prepare her to act at the right time at the right place. Her suffering fulfilled God's plan, and taught her to trust in God even when it seemed illogical and *unprofitable*.

Each of these *heroes* learned from their suffering that God was greater than they had previously understood – an also learned that their heroism was merely God working through them. Each of them went from knowing *about* God to knowing him more fully. And each found greater joy and contentment through the process.

We could go on. God often uses suffering and situations in which it would be *understandable* for the person experiencing it to consider the possibility that God had abandoned them - but through it all the Father *is there* and is growing the sufferer's faith. God is there in the suffering and the pain the person goes through enables them to see him more clearly and gloriously than they ever had before. They are transformed through the experience. Perhaps suffering is *the best* catalyst for spiritual growth.

The Apostle Paul put it this way:

> *Not only that, but we rejoice in our sufferings, knowing that suffering produces endurance, and endurance produces character, and character produces hope, and hope does not put us to shame, because God's love has been poured into our hearts through the Holy Spirit who has been given to us.*[101]

God thought very highly of Job so he wanted to give him a precious gift - an even greater faith. He used Satan's foolish wager to accomplish that.

I doubt Job would have traded the wonderful gift that God delivered through suffering for anything in the world.

Application: When you find yourself in hard circumstances and suffering, trust that God is working even if you cannot understand the plan.

2. **When in fear, when in doubt, when in pain – choose to trust God.**

This seems obvious when things are going well for us. But when our world starts falling apart, it is easy to lose sight of. Just like Job, although perhaps to a lesser degree, does it not seem that at certain times our troubles and challenges all mount up at once? As the days of trouble draw out into weeks, months, and sometimes years, we can easily begin to question, "God, where are you? How can you let this happen?"

What would Job tell us in such a time?

First of all, he would definitely understand our doubts and confusion. We are creatures with limited and varying abilities to handle grief and sorrow. When we get overwhelmed, we may lash out at God, reject him, say hurtful things to others, and lose hope.

Is it okay to *curse* God? This is the second thing I believe Job would share – I perceive he might gently say, *"I wish I hadn't, but God can handle it."* Our Creator loves us more than we can comprehend – and this *love* is not the feelings-based fuzzy modern concept of love so popular today. It is a love that seeks our best no matter what. We must know, then, that when we hurt that God *hurts with us*. But without that pain, we cannot receive the gift of greater faith – and the resultant joy.

So when we are hurt, discouraged, and unsure of the plan, what should we do? Perhaps Job would recommend that we just tell God that *we are hurt, discouraged, and unsure of the plan.*

A few years ago I found myself as a military pilot in the deserts of the Middle East during the Second Gulf War. As we left our home base, I was sure God was going to do some amazing things in and through me during this trial. But within a few months I found myself quite disillusioned and confused. Most of the war that I was involved in was an intra-military political farce. It became clear that nearly every senior officer was primarily concerned about getting promoted and earning medals rather than supporting the war and taking care of the men in their command. This is something I have little patience for, because in the process they were risking the lives of the people I cared for – my squadron mates in particular.

Further, we for the most part were just spinning our wheels. We flew long days in difficult conditions facing threats from missiles and small-arms fire – all while normally flying *empty airplanes!* The primary purpose of all of our exposure to wartime threats, being separated from family and friends, and using public resources was to better the careers of numerous senior military officers. I was infuriated.

I remember one day walking along after a particularly bad encounter with one of my superior officers over this grandstanding of theirs – walking in the 120-degree heat, and talking to God. I was very unhappy, and a doubt came to my mind as I walked; "What if he doesn't care? What if he isn't even there?"

I do not know if the voice was from Satan or just my own selfish weakness, but the story of Job came to mind. I had poured over the story for so long and taught it as a class at church several times – and I knew what Job would have me do.

I looked toward the hot sky, with tears forming in my eyes, missing my family and hating my current situation, and I stated *out loud* to my Father:

Lord, I don't like this and I don't get what you are doing. But I trust you are doing something. I will hang on to you with every ounce of strength I have!"

From that day forward, God changed my heart. I found enjoyment and purpose in each day. Do not get me wrong, nothing changed in the war. *God changed my heart.* I stopped trying to make sense of everything I didn't understand and looked for what I could do that God showed me, and I tried to do it well and with a good attitude. I did eventually see the plan, and it was grander and more personal than I ever would have imagined!

I started experiencing joy again.

Application: When you don't understand what God is doing and are tempted to lash out, just let God know you trust him anyway and move on in faith.

3.   God will succeed in all of his plans through his strength.

This may almost see redundant in light of the last truth, but it is true nonetheless.

Job may have seen his response as a failure. He was tested by Satan, with God's permission, and did exactly what Satan said he would do!

Was this an epic failure?

No, God accomplished what he set out to do, *using Job.* Satan was *ultimately attacking the character of God*, and Job's cursing demonstrated that God was loving, compassionate, merciful, loyal, and forgiving.

Job cursed.

Satan got what he wanted.

Satan lost the wager.

God succeeded in his plan.

Job did not have to respond perfectly, but he did need to stand firm with God. This is what he in fact did. He never rejected or left God, he just *cursed* God in his pain, weakness, and limited understanding.

The Almighty's plan of showing his own faithfulness in the face of our weakness succeeded.

God wins every time. This wager involved Job, but was not *about* Job. It was about the Almighty – he won. He always wins.

Applying Truth Three – God succeeding in his plans is not dependent on our perfection – it is reliant on his perfection! The pressure is off.

4.   **God's children sometimes suffer because they are God's children.**

Eliphaz, Bildad, and Zophar were convicted in their hearts that Job was suffering because of unconfessed sin.

The truth was, Job was suffering because he was a faithful child of God.

As has been pointed out by many, we do not live on a playground, *we live on a battleground*. And as our Lord is the commander of the army, there are times when we will suffer attack *because* we are his troops.

When Jesus sent out his 12 men to the lost people of Israel, his words might seem, well, discouraging:

> *Look, I am sending you out as sheep among the wolves...you will handed over to the courts and flogged with whips in the synagogues...you will stand trial before governors and kings because you are my followers...when you are arrested...all*

nations will hate you because you are my followers.[102]

It doesn't seem like a very good sales job on Jesus' part. But it was *real.* When we put on Christ and live by his power, the light of his righteousness causes some to be uncomfortable. Seeing the beauty of Christ in someone also causes the contrasting ugliness of evil to be shown for what it is in others – and people become angry. They lash out, call us names, cause harm, and may even kill us. Satan is behind all of this – for just as in the story of Job, loyalty to God infuriates the adversary of God.

He will come after you – because you are following the Christ.

Jesus has an answer to that in the same message he gave to his 12 travelling ambassadors:

> *Don't be afraid of those who want to kill your body; they cannot touch your soul. Fear only God, who can destroy both body and soul in hell. What is the price of two sparrows – one copper coin? But not a single sparrow can fall to the ground without your Father knowing it. And the very hairs on your head are all numbered. So don't be afraid; you are more valuable to God than a whole flock of sparrows.*[103]

Our Lord knows so well what we are like – we do not *want* to suffer. But he wants us to know that because we do live on a battleground, suffering *will* come. And in that moment when it touches each of us, we must *rely upon him* to give us the strength to stand firm in our Savior's grace. We may not understand on this side of heaven *why* the trial has come – but we can hear the voice of Job through the ages speak truth to us:

> *...No purpose of yours can be thwarted.*[104]

In dramatic contrast to what Eliphaz, Bildad, and Zophar contended – that Job was suffering because he did something wrong, we must remember the lesson of this truth:

Application: When things seem tough and we are suffering, it may be because we are doing what is right! Stand firm and trust God.

5. **When facing hardship and doubt, give God the benefit of the doubt.**

If we dare to imagine more of what Job's advice would be to us today when things are good or especially when times are tough, I perceive he might say, "Trust God no matter what."

With the background information shared with us in the written word, we are blessed with an insight to the horrible persecution of Job based upon the wager of Satan. *But Job had no way of knowing this when he was in the moment.* This was what was so confusing to him given his incomplete and partially idolatrous view of God.

But once he experienced God himself, and interestingly *not the story that we are privy to,* everything was suddenly "too wonderful." Job discovered when enveloped in the presence of God that *who* God is was a sufficient reason to endure any *what.* In the incredible, overwhelming presence of God, Job intuitively understood that God could be trusted – and I think he would gently encourage us to do the same *if possible!*

When we are under stress and pain and we happen to slip up and lash out at God, he is more than capable of taking it – he made us and does know that we are weak.

When in doubt, fear, uncertainty, and desiring comfort – let your Father know about it. But also endeavor to let him hear the words, "I hurt, but I trust you."

Application: At all times and in all circumstances, endeavor to hold on to God and let him know that you trust his heart.

6. **We may not enjoy his plan; humility and steadfastness are needed.**

I have some very sweet friends who love God. And on more than one occasion I have heard one of them say, "If you are in God's will, you will have a sense of peace."

It sounds so beautiful. It is what we want to hear. It reinforces the view of God we want to hold. If I am doing what is right, he will let me know by giving me peace in my life.

Job calls that idea into question as does much of the rest of the Bible. We've already seen and can imagine the horrors of the emotions Job endured following the attack of Satan. Yet he was in the *very center of where God wanted him to be*. Let's look at another notable God-lover who found himself in the center of God's will, yet likely found a sense of peace challenging to maintain.

A king of Judah named Asa had been blessed with peace and wisdom early in his reign. He receives notice that Zerah the Ethiopian is heading his way with a conquering army. It's not just any army though, Zerah's army outnumbers Asa's by nearly two-to-one, and he has 300 chariots. Asa rouses his much-smaller force with *no chariots* and rushes out to meet this overwhelming force. He draws up his men in battle formation, and says this:

> *O LORD, no one but you can help the powerless against the mighty! Help us,*
> *O LORD our God, for we trust in you alone. It is in your name that we have come*

against this vast horde. O LORD, you are our God; do not let mere men prevail against you![105]

Think not only of King Asa, but perhaps the majority of his 580,000 warriors. They are lined up for battle and the enemy they are facing is intimidating and just plain huge! Each man under Asa's command must kill about 2 men on his own, or at least get them to run away and stop fighting in order to prevail. And then they hear Asa praying right before the battle is engaged. It isn't necessarily what you want to hear, for he pretty much says, "Lord, unless you show up, we will die."

Asa is pretty certain the men under his command are doomed – not something that would inspire confidence or a sense of peace.

These men may not have been enjoying this plan of God. They couldn't say, "Oh hey, we can take them!" They were outnumbered and outgunned. Facing chariots with nothing but "shields and spears"[106] would be akin an army without helicopters and attack aircraft facing another army that had them – it is daunting. When those chariots would blaze through their midst at high speed, highly armored and with strong warriors bearing sharp swords and spears – it would be a very difficult battle to win on foot.

I don't think Asa's army was enjoying the moment before the battle began. I doubt many of them had a *sense of peace*. A sense of foreboding would have been very understandable. It looked like a dreadful defeat was brewing.

But oh, the moment when Zerah and what was left of his army began to flee in terror before the LORD[107]; would not that have been awesome! The joy and awe came *after* a period of fear and dread. Asa and his fighting men had to stand in spite of their lack of ability to see victory.

Just know that in our life walking with God, there will be times when God's plan, as it unfolds around us, will make us *very* uncomfortable. While God's plans are always there and always good, we may not feel that sense of peace that my friends claim we will possess if we are in the center of God's plan.

Steadfastness or perseverance is the quality of choosing beforehand to stand with God even if it costs you your life. It is based upon abiding in God through his word and his presence daily in order to *know* that *he can be trusted*, and then making our *covenant* with him to do so no matter what.

Humility is required. If we are to stand when we cannot understand what God is doing, we will have to trust that our God will triumph *even when we cannot*, with our best reason and emotions, comprehend why things are happening as they are. We must fully own the truth that Isaiah spoke from the Almighty:

> *"My thoughts are nothing like your thoughts," says the LORD. "And my ways are far beyond anything you could imagine. For just as the heavens are higher than the earth, so my ways are higher than your ways and my thoughts higher than your thoughts.*[108]

How often today do we hear someone, or perhaps hear *ourselves* say something along the line of, "Well, I think God would want me to...", and then pronounce a self-reasoned rationale as to why what Scripture clearly says *does not apply to us?*

Isn't it true that in such rationalizing we are stating that in view of our great wisdom, the very clear Word of God does not apply? Is this not *hubris,* excessive self-pride or confidence? Negating what our Creator has instructed us to do based upon our intellectualism or a desire to bend to popular opinion is the opposite of humility – and it will stand in the way of God working his plans through us.

In fact, pushing aside the distinct guidance of God for our own reasoned ideas is idolatry. We have enthroned and are bowing down before a god made *in our own image* – and it is a horrible sin.

But what a blessing we can experience, as Job and Asa found out, if we will endure through the trial and see God victorious in his plan – *as he always is*. If we will let God stay on his throne and keep his precepts even when we do not understand or enjoy what is going on – then God is glorified (as he should be) and we can take part in his victory triumph! The Apostle Paul put it this way:

> *Therefore take up the whole armor of God, that you may be able to withstand in the evil day, and having done all, to stand firm.*[109]

Application: Just because things look and feel bad does not mean things are not going the way they are supposed to. Being in the center of God's will may at times place us in moments of great fear, doubt, pain, and loss. But wait for it, perseverance (steadfastness) is rewarded in the end with victory. Stand firm in the faith when facing trials.

7.   When God says, "I am with you always," He means it.

It may seem like I am beating a dead horse here, but if you were able to read the account of Job and put yourself in his place, can you imagine how alone or abandoned Job must have felt? How could God be in the situation he faced? All he could conceive was that God had made an error and was harming him.

Not only can we sometimes feel that God has abandoned us, when we strive to serve God we sometimes feel as though we are the only human alive that still cares about God.

The prophet Elijah of the Old Testament had his moments of loneliness. After experiencing the amazing victory of God over the false prophets of Baal, Queen Jezebel set her forces in hot pursuit to kill him. She was a worshipper of this imaginary god, and was raging with anger over what God had done through Elijah.

Elijah took off running. First, he prays that God would take his life.[110] Then he went to Mount Sinai and hid in a cave. The LORD comes to him and asks:

"What are you doing here Elijah?"[111]

Elijah answers:

> *I have zealously served the LORD God Almighty. But the people of Israel have broken their covenant with you, torn down your altars, and killed every one of your prophets. I am the only one left, and now they are trying to kill me, too.*[112]

It would be profitable to go back and read the whole story[113] leading up to this. This man who is running from the infamous Queen Jezebel had just stood up to King Ahab, 450 prophets of the false god Baal, and the 400 prophets of the false goddess Asherah. He had stood alone in front of all Israel and challenged, mocked, and stood strong while the prophets of the man-made gods made fools of themselves. They danced, prayed, shouted, cried, and cut themselves trying to get their imaginary gods to burn up the animals on their altar.

When they failed, Elijah had his altar soaked with water, said a simple prayer, and a fire from heaven fell upon the altar and absolutely devoured the sacrifice and vaporized the water. Every witness fell on their faces in fear of the power of the One True God!

And yet immediately after this amazing display of God's power that Elijah *experienced,* he suddenly hits a vicious low. There is a strong lesson here in our limitations as created beings – the famous WWII U.S. Army General George Patton had learned this limitation well and put it in his usual colorful style:

> *Life is like a roller-coaster. Life has its ups and downs. I've been up and down many times. Every time I get an award or win or a victory, I expect to be shot at by enemies – even by friends... so when you ride this roller coaster of life to a high point, always be prepared for the down slope.*[114]

While it seems difficult to conceive that Elijah, after seeing such an amazing example of the power of God working based upon his simple prayer, would so shortly be running for fear of his life, feeling alone, and ready to die – yet there it is. God preserved this very *human* example of one of the heroes of the Bible experiencing what is a common problem for all of us mortal creatures. We can and will become totally discouraged at the most unlikely (and likely) times. What is the antidote?

As common as the problem is, the message of encouragement is found throughout his Word. Here is what he said to Elijah when he was hiding in the cave:

> *Go back the same way you came...anoint Hazael to be king of Aram...anoint Jehu...to be king of Israel...anoint Elisha...to replace you as prophet...I will preserve 7,000 others in Israel who have never bowed down to Baal or kissed him!*[115]

Let's unpack what God told Elijah, and understand how it applies to us when we are on the downslopes of Patton's rollercoaster.

First, when we are discouraged, lonely, and feeling abandoned, *go back!* For Elijah, this was a physical journey, but for you it may mean more of mental/spiritual trek. If you feel that God is not around, that perception is likely is not true! If he is not near you, it is you who have wondered off! Much like the story of the wayward or "prodigal" son, the son left the father, but the father was searching for his son and ran to him when he saw him.[116] So if you have followed your own way, just head back toward your Father and he will come running to meet you!

Or, if you just *feel* alone because you are miserable, persecuted, unsure, lonely, or you are not understanding what is happening – just realize that your Lord is *very near.* We don't have to like what is happening, *just tell him you do not like it.* We do not have to understand or agree with what is happening, we just need to tell him we trust him in spite of our limitations.

Just as a young child who is scared will place their arms up and cry for their mommy or daddy, so should we cry out to our *Abba* Father when we are hurt, scared, confused, or lonely. He is there.

He. Is. There.

We need to cry out for help, and let him know that we cannot do it without him. And we should endeavor to send the words from our mouth, "I will not let go of you, Father, please grant me strength to hold on!"

Application: We as created beings will have very low times in our lives when we have doubt, pain, confusion, fear, and feel all alone. These times may follow immediately after a great victory or time of high faith. We must look past our feelings and trust that when our Savior the Christ said, "I will be with you, always,"[117] he meant that he would be with us, always. He meant it.

8. Satan is more vicious than you ever imagined.

It has become more publicly acceptable in recent decades to *come out* as a proponent or adherent to Satan-worship, witchcraft, or a member of a Pagan religion. You might say that we've softened Satan's image in this day of tolerance.

But for an accurate view of who the Adversary is, we only need to return to the account of what exactly happened during the two days God let Satan do what he wished *nearly unrestrained.* He destroyed *all* of Job's possessions. He snuffed out *all* of Job's children. He covered Job in severe boils from the soles of his head to the crown of his head.

All for what?

Just to bring someone down into the pit he was already in!

Do not ever let your guard down about the pointless and cruel evil Satan thrives on. Stay close to God through his word, prayer, and his people. Never. Let. Go.

Application: Satan is a formidable and vicious foe of everything truly good. We must abide in God through his word, prayer, and his people.

9. God is the hero of the story, always.

I believe Job would passionately urge us to take this lesson away from his story – the hero of the story was God the Almighty, not Job. We have access and power to do amazing things in the Kingdom of God in the same manner that Job did. It is not up to us to power our way into excellence in order to be pleasing to God. Our Creator is *pleased with us* and will work through us in his power if we trust him and stand firm.

Mary, the mother of Jesus, shows how to handle the heroic nature of God when he works in our lives. She too was given a difficult assignment, given the nature of her role in it. You could very well say that God's plan for Mary and the world wasn't just hard to understand, it was *incomprehensible.*

She, a virgin betrothed to a good man, would suddenly be pregnant. When the inevitable question arose from her father, or friends, of "Who did this to you," her answer would have seemed *blasphemous.* Imagine a young Jewish girl answering that very normal question with the absurd truth; "Oh, God did this. The LORD got me pregnant."

We could easily understand if the men in town had picked up rocks *immediately* to stone her to death! That is not the way God does things! When in the history of the world had God gotten a young girl pregnant? *Never!*

But yet in Mary's case, the Holy Spirit brought about life within the womb of *this* young lady. And through that life came the great news of salvation for the entire world!

What did Mary have to say about her role in God's plan when she was with someone who would comprehend it? It is beautiful, humble, and full of praise:

> *Oh, how my soul praises the Lord. How my spirit rejoices in God my Savior! For he took notice of his lowly servant girl, and from now on all generations will call me blessed. For the Mighty One is holy, and he has done great things for me.*

I have always been so moved by her initial response to the angel's message that she would bear the Messiah[118] and become pregnant *before she was married.* As many through the years have pointed out, this was potentially a death sentence for Mary. To be found pregnant and not married was cause for stoning. At the very best, she would be ostracized by those she was closest too. The chances that even God-fearing people would believe that God would impregnate a young girl are slim. It would just seem like a very insulting accusation against God to justify her own bad behavior with some other guy.

Back to her response, she had to know this *plan* of the Almighty would not make sense to anyone around her. She simply has one question before she gave her answer:

But how can this happen? I am a virgin.[119]

She doesn't resist the plan, she just has the very natural problem with *how she will become pregnant.* Her question seems to be, *will the baby be mine and Josephs', or is something or someone else going to get me pregnant?* If it is to be that the Messiah is going to be the product of the physical union of the man she is betrothed to, then that isn't so bad.

But God's plan was the less desirable option from a social standpoint. She would be pregnant without a man – something *nobody* was likely to believe.

Joseph was an honorable man, but would he even believe her.

But nonetheless, she gave her answer to the angel, the answer that still brings tears to my eyes and motivates me in my service to my Maker:

I am the Lord's servant. May everything you have said about me come true.[120]

Mary, like Job, was pretty much along for the ride in the cosmic war between the

Almighty Creator and his rebellious creature Satan. Every moment of her future life was vested in the Lord of Creation *showing up and protecting her while he carried out his plan.*

And so her words of praise for her hero are even more touching given this truth.

For the Mighty One has done great things for me![121]

I am convicted that Job would have sung the same song with her! For in that moment on the ash heap of his life, he experienced the overwhelming presence of God – and every earthly worry faded away into the beautiful and all-encompassing presence of the glory of God.

The hero was, and is, and always shall be our Creator!

Application: Our Lord delights in us and in doing great things through us – let us always praise him and let the world know he is the majestic and loving God who deserves our praise!

10. Experiencing God *will Transform Who You Are!*

The last truth leads into this one, but *no one* can *experience* the holiness of the Mighty One of heaven and *not be transformed!* If we seek God and he progressively shows us who he truly is, we will be amazed, awed, and overwhelmed. We will find that we must act; either we will draw close and find our lives changed forever, subsumed in his will, or, we will absolutely reject him and enthrone ourselves as deity.

As was mentioned in an earlier chapter regarding Moses, we are not capable of taking in all of God's glory at once. The Almighty himself told Moses that to do so would be so overwhelming it would kill him. And so we must continually choose to *abide* in God. We must purpose to set aside inviolate times in which we sit with him, with his Word, and we humbly ask Him to reveal himself to us. We must study and dwell in the Word, with an attitude of expectancy, that the Holy Spirit will direct our heart and minds into a greater intimacy with our Maker. We must be alert as we walk with him in his world, and let him teach us in the various ways he will. Through interactions with others, through the environment, and through the Holy Spirit – we may grow in a greater knowledge of the awesomeness of God – and be transformed.

But we must, as in any relationship, be deliberate in our actions. Once when the Lord was speaking through Jeremiah he voiced a principle that I perceive he still honors with his people today:

In those days when you pray, I will listen. If you look for me wholeheartedly, you will find me. I will be found by you...[122]

The Apostle Paul put it this way:

Don't copy the behavior and customs of this world, but let God transform you into a new person by changing the way you think. Then you will learn to know God's will for you, which is good and pleasing and perfect.[123]

For me, this is *the biggest moment in the whole account of Job.* The most transformative moment for this pitiful suffering man comes while he is *in the very midst of our Father, and he states that in his suffering, he had talked of things "too wonderful for me."*[124] Do not let this slip past you; this is, I contend, the most important moment in the story.

Job lost almost everything that a person would value in the world, except for his wife and his life. He lost it with shocking suddenness. He rails at God, understandably. He believes fervently that God has made an error and is dealing with him wrongly – and who can blame him? It was clear that the power capable of orchestrating such destruction would have to be other-worldly, and Job only knew One who was powerful enough. It was natural to blame God and to be furiously angry at the injustice.

And then, in a matter of minutes, this same tortured man is suddenly repentant and speaking of thing "too wonderful for me, which I did not know."[125]

Going back to Paul's words above, Job experienced one of the most radical changes in thinking perhaps ever seen. He went from being engulfed in sorrow and anger to being full of wonder and praise.

Just like that.

Transformed, utterly and completely.

And so, in my life, I want to be transformed – to take part in the joy of serving God with absolute courage and enthusiasm.

Job tells us, something like that will occur when we see God more accurately as he is.

Application: In order to be transformed into a mighty man or woman of God, we must increasingly see God for Who he truly is. We must experience in increasing measure his power, glory, love, justice, and presence. This will take our choosing to pursue him daily, and a willingness to stand with him when things do not make sense.

PART II

OTHER FAITH LESSONS

Chapter 8

The Unnamed One Speaks

If Job's response was less than perfect, as were his friends, wouldn't it be handy to know what a better response would have been?

Did you know that there is one person who did respond well to the challenges that Job faced?

Do you know who it was?

Would you like to know?

Train Like We Fight

One of the great lessons of the military, sports, and aviation is that training for future tough events is best accomplished by simulating those events to the most realistic degree safely possible. Then from that experience, we can adopt a mental model of *what to do* when stress and emotions *would tend to make us react poorly instead of properly.* This is called the principle of *train like we fight.*

Fortunately, there is one person in the story of Job who actually does say what is right. Would you like to know how to prepare your mind and heart for virtually any challenge in life? Would you like to know the secret to handling great times and bad times?

There is one unlikely person in this cast of characters in the story of Job who shares with us the proper way to deal with any situation in life, especially the grueling and confusing ones. We can study and meditate on what this one person says to better prepare ourselves for whatever comes our way in life.

The Unimportant, Unnamed One

Whoever recorded Job's story lets us know about all of the players. There is God, the angels, Satan, Job, Job's 10-children, and Job's wife. Then Satan is allowed to attack twice, and at some point, Eliphaz, Bildad, and Zophar show up and sit with Job.

But there is someone else sitting there with this crew. Whether he showed up before, with or after the three friends isn't mentioned.

Apparently he is not mentioned, because, according to his own words, he is younger. This is a society that highly values age and wisdom, so this mystery guest just did not make the cut. He was not important enough to be mentioned.

But he suddenly becomes important when his words explode into the conversation. The writer introduces him in this way:

> *Then Elihu the son of Barachel the Buzite, of the family of Ram, burned with anger. He burned with anger at Job because he justified himself rather than God. He burned with anger also at Job's three friends because they had found no answer, although they had declared Job to be in the wrong. Now Elihu had waited to speak to Job because they were older than he. And when Elihu saw that there was no answer in the mouth of these three men, he burned with anger.*[126]

What is fascinating about Elihu is not just that he is not mentioned although he was sitting there the whole time. There is more, much more; Elihu bears a unique distinction amongst those who have many words to say. Elihu, when he speaks, carries on for six continuous chapters once he gets started. So he speaks just as much or more as anyone else in the story.

But he is unique when it is all over in one particular regard.

He receives no condemnation from God. *None.*

As we saw earlier, God has some strong words for Job:

Who is this that darkens counsel by words without knowledge?[127]

He has frightening words for Eliphaz, Bildad, and Zophar:

> *My anger burns against you and against your two friends, for you have not spoken of me what is right...*[128]

But for Eliphaz, God has nothing. Not one mention of Eliphaz or the things he brought up.

Would you like to know what the right things to say are in any demanding situation? Let us look at some of the dominant themes Eliphaz the younger teaches us.

Remember Who You Are, and Whose You Are

Eliphaz begins somewhat apologetically discussing why he hasn't responded but now why he must. And when he gets rolling with his words, the first point he makes is this:

The Spirit of God has made me, and the breath of the Almighty gives me life...Behold, I am toward God as you are; I too was pinched off from a piece of clay.

It is good to remember, as some in the south say, that we *shouldn't get too big for our britches!* Elihu is furious with Job making much of himself by insulting the righteousness and justice of God. In this initial statement, he reminds Job (and us) that the sovereign Creator and Lord of all that is *made us.* We are ultimately his, even though he gives us the freedom to do as we please for a while. But ultimately, we are created beings, and we belong to God. He *can* do as he needs to do with us. As Job was soon to admit, God has a *purpose* which cannot be prevented, and so it is good to remember that we may not always enjoy our life, but ultimately, *we do belong to God*. He made us, he owns us, and we should never forget this!

The Apostle Paul several centuries later would give us this word picture of the principle Elihu taught:

> *But who are you, O man, to answer back to God? Will what is molded say to its molder, 'Why have you made me like this?' Has the potter no right over the clay, to make out of the same lump one vessel for honorable use and another for dishonorable use?*[129]

On the day I began writing this chapter, a very dear lady who has been a friend of my wife and me for more than two decades was diagnosed with multiple myeloma. This rare blood cancer is treatable but not curable. This lady has always been such a sweet and encouraging believer – her diagnosis follows years of pain and confusion as to what was going on in her small body. It hurts me to think about what she must go through now – but go through it she must.

It is natural to have that feeling within, and look toward God and ask, "Why her?" She is such a small lady, so sweet, so full of praise for God – why is she being singled out for this suffering?

Elihu's words are hard, but right. We are all pinched off from a piece of clay. We all are part of God's plan. Who am I to question what God needs to do with what is his? Further, what might he need to do with me?

Our sufferings, challenges, and confusion here on earth are complex and can be so painful. But we will eventually meet our Maker – and I would contend from what Job learned that at the moment we do, everything will be fantastic! Meeting God will be the ultimate moment of clarity.

Let us remember that we are created beings, the prized property of the awesome Creator! We do not have to understand what is going on in order to know that he owns it all. We can and must trust his heart.

God is Greater than Man

Elihu begins his next thought by quoting Job:

> You [Job] say, 'I am pure, without transgression; I am clean, and there is no iniquity in me. Behold he finds occasion against me, he counts me as his enemy, he puts my feet in the stocks, and watches all my paths.'[130]

Elihu's answer to Job's contention is simple but profound.

"Wrong."

That's my paraphrase, his exact words are as follows:

Behold, in this you are not right. I will answer you, for God is greater than man.[131]

This might *seem* obvious, but *anytime* we find ourselves being critical of God, his actions, or our perceptions of his actions, are we not placing ourselves on a higher throne than his?

While it is perfectly natural to struggle with what we experience in life and not understand what God is doing, we should always remember that *God is greater!*

Our limitations of comprehension do not justify our criticism or our condemnation of God's character.

God is greater than me.

Job fully perceives this sense of the greatness once he *experiences* the presence and glory of the Almighty. What is interesting is that young *Elihu has this in his heart before God shows up.* What was it in Elihu's daily practice toward God that kept the glory, holiness, power and majesty of God before him with such clarity?

Perhaps it would be helpful when we have our daily sit-down with God to spend some time praising him properly. When we sing songs and say words indicating God's greatness and goodness, we are not telling him anything he does not know – but are we not informing our own hearts? If we are together with our church family engaged in praise, are we not teaching one another through our praise that *God is indeed greater than us?*

Reading the story of the prophet Isaiah's vision of God on the throne may help us as well. Isaiah was an amazing follower of God, and much like Job nothing bad is really ever said about him. Yet in one experience that he had, when he was allowed to see the Lord on his throne, "high and lifted up,"[132] what he perceived even as a righteous man shook him to the core of his being.

He sees angelic creatures flying around our God, praising God for his holiness. He

heard a voice that shook the foundations of the heavenly temple in which the Lord sat –
and in all of his amazement, he perceived one thing as he *experienced* the magnitude of
who God was and is:

> *Woe is me! For I am lost; for I am a man of unclean lips, and I dwell in the midst*
> *of a people of unclean lips; for my eyes have seen the King, the LORD of hosts!*[133]

Both Job and Isaiah were remarkably faithful *men;* but when they experienced
the greatness and presence of God, they both had their entire attitude toward God
transformed. All either one of them could see in the presence of God was their own sin,
and the magnificent perfect holiness of God.

They saw that God was greater.

In our own walk with God, it would be good for us to examine those times when
created beings such as ourselves encountered God in his glory. We need to prayerfully
ask God to keep before us his majesty, so that we too, like Elihu, can remember that *God*
is indeed greater than we are, amazingly greater!

God Answers, even if You do not Perceive it.

Throughout Job's speaking prior to the appearance of God, he complains of not being
heard. Elihu speaks Job's words back to him:

Why do you contend against him, saying, 'He will answer none of man's words?'

Elihu has an answer to this idea of God not answering, and it is challenging to us:

For God speaks again and again, though people do not realize it.[134]

He goes on to talk about God specifically speaking or teaching through dreams or through experiences (such as pain being a rebuke); he does not claim to have all the answers, but he is fully convicted that God does answer us in ways that perhaps we simply do not or cannot comprehend at times.

Elihu seems uncertain, from the things he says in this section of the story, whether or not Job had sinned or not. He does not accuse Job as the other friends of Job do. He is just fully confident that the God that he knows personally does not callously turn his head away from his children when they speak.

He contends that the problem instead is *you and me.*

We are not attentive to God. We sometimes do not hear because we do not like the answer.

I do not know what the attitude of people in the days of Elihu were towards God. But I think his contention that we are not attentive towards the Almighty is truer in today's American culture than ever. Albert Mohler lamented "The larger scandal is biblical ignorance among Christians. Choose whatever statistic or survey you like; the general pattern is the same. America's Christians know less and less about the Bible. It shows."[135]

Recent surveys show the average American spends 24 hours *per week online.*[136] That is one full day of the life that God gave primarily engaged in something that has very little eternal consequence.

Additionally, as a nation we also spend a daily average of 8 hours and 55 minutes watching television.[137] Obviously some of this screen time happens concurrently with other activities – but when one considers time spent at school, work, or sleeping – exactly how much time does the average believer in God actually spend *listening to God through time in the Bible?*

For God speaks in one way, and in two, though man does not perceive it.[138]

We will not likely perceive or hide the word of the Almighty in our hearts and minds if we are being indoctrinated by secular sources on the internet and television for more than half of our waking time.

One of the most profound ways in which God speaks to us and prepares us to handle life is through the inspired Word. We can claim to love God, but if we do not value his Word to us enough to spend time daily reading, meditating, praying, *and memorizing* His conversation with us — can we truly claim that *love?*

This lack of daily substantial time with God also creates another problem. I have heard many believers claiming to have heard a *word from the Holy Spirit.* But how does one know something we perceive is from the Holy Spirit actually is from God? The one thing we must be able to do in order to determine whether or not something is from God is to know the written Word of God *intimately*. The Holy Spirit is not the only spiritual being out there! God (the Holy Spirit) cannot contradict the Word he has already given. We must have a complete familiarity with the entire word of God, or *the whole counsel of God* as saints of the past called it, in order to correctly determine whether or not what we perceive is of the Holy Spirit or from the deceiver himself!

If we as believers would be strong and ready to handle any challenge, good or bad, in life — we must make *time with God a priority, not time with a screen!* Elihu has a remarkably vibrant vision of God, in spite of his relative youth. I suspect that did not happen by accident.

If we are to know in our hearts that God is greater than us, we must spend time with him each day

God's Desire is to Save and Impart the Light of Life

This thought runs intertwined with the previous about the truth that God does listen and does respond, even if we are not able to perceive it.

I get the impression that Elihu has some suspicions as to *why* Job is suffering, but is honestly confused. What he does insist on though is the holiness and absolute purity of God's heart. Elihu's discourse is an unrestrained and passionate defense of his Creator. Unlike Job's other friends, he does not claim to have God's knowledge of Job's problems – but he does know that God is absolutely good.

In Chapter 33, beginning with the discussion about God speaking even if man doesn't hear it (verse 14 and following), he says something that would have possibly sounded shocking to those who knew Job:

> *He [God] speaks in dreams, in visions of the night, when deep sleep falls on people as they lie in their beds. He whispers in their ears and terrifies them with warnings. He makes them turn from doing wrong;* ***he keeps them from pride.***[139]

Was Elihu informed of Job's pride by the Holy Spirit, or was it just the natural observation of Job being righteous in his own eyes while condemning God as being in the wrong?

As was discussed in an earlier chapter, the wager of Satan was *without reason,* but we perceive the possibility that God had a great purpose in mind, one that does *keep Job from pride* and increases his faith in an amazing way.

Job's pride is not *hubris,* that being excessive pride or confidence based upon one's abilities, rather it seems to be perceiving oneself to know more about God and being a *good person* almost to the level of perfection. Job was living out a beautiful vibrant faith in his community and likely was showered with praise for doing so. People sought him out for spiritual advice.

I do not think it is at all likely that Job believed himself to be sinless – he was well familiar and engaged in the process of the atonement sacrifice, as demonstrated with those he made after each of his children's parties. But when this famous trial fell upon Job, he knew that he was *in the right* and that God had made a huge mistake.

He had God figured out.

Only it turns out, that although Job was a noteworthy man of faith, *there was still room for growth.* And this is one of the reasons why God allowed Job to undergo such an excruciating ordeal – Job *was* a man of tremendous faith, but in order to grow to the next level, he needed to experience God at a level he had not been ready for earlier. God did indeed, as Elihu was musing, want to show Job "the light of life."[140]

In that moment after just about everything Job valued was brutally stripped from him, and after having a week to think it over and decide God was at fault – when God shows up in the whirlwind and Job is confronted *with the beautiful and awesome other-ness of The Almighty, he was transfixed and transformed by the light of life.* Job's choosing of the words "too wonderful"[141] should be considered in the light of the truest sense of the word.

We do live in an age of spectacle – we see amazing things brought to us through various media platforms. We can watch movies of alien invasions or of stories about imaginary worlds that look as real as the theatre or home we are sitting in. It used to be that people would say, "seeing is believing." It is no longer true – computer graphics and manipulation of imagery have deadened us to believing even what we see. Sadly, they have also killed our sense of wonder.

Job was living an intense life. He was wealthy, had a lot going on, and was needed and valued in his village. He was likely busy nearly every moment of the day, working, helping people, loving his family, and loving God.

But when God agreed to the wager and all of Job's busy-ness came to a sudden halt, the time was right for the Almighty to do for Job something of incredible beauty. In the stillness and desolation of intense suffering and depravation, Job's Creator comes to earth, and shows his suffering child just a smidgen of the glory that is our God – and this act of extreme love changes Job's view of God and of life itself forever. He saw the light:

> *I had heard of you by the hearing of the ear, but now my eye sees you;*
>
> *therefore I despise myself, and repent in dust and ashes.*[142]

Do you know what is really remarkable about this statement of Job? Elihu *predicted* it! In Elihu's musings on the way in which God speaks, he said this about what happens when the Lord finally reaches his mark in the human heart:

> *...Man prays to God, and he accepts him; he sees his face **with a shout of joy**,*
>
> *and he restores to man his righteousness. He sings before men and says: '**I sinned***
>
> ***and perverted what was right**, and it was not repaid me. He has redeemed my*
>
> *soul from going down into the pit, and my life shall look upon the light.*[143]

Elihu's wisdom teach us something about who we *could* be in God. It isn't always older believers who are the most zealous and wise. It is those who diligently seek the Lord and who are determined to defend his greatness who can be the most remarkable. Elihu hits a lot of things straight on and righteously.

Job does indeed *shout for joy,* as far as speaking of things too wonderful in light of all he had lost. He does admit his sin – "I despise myself and repent in dust and ashes."[144]

Yet what many students of the Word have struggled with is the *nature of Job's sin.*

Eliphaz, Bildad, and Zophar got it wrong. Job had not been defrauding, abusing, or otherwise harming others.

Job's sin was more complicated, perhaps we might say more *advanced.* He presumed too much in his knowledge of the Holy One. He had too high an opinion of his own goodness and too low a view of the Creator. He dared to *justify himself rather than God,*[145] which was the very thing that infuriated Elihu so much!

Do you do the same? Do you have too high an opinion of your own opinion? Do you question God's judgment, righteousness, and actions? Do you presume that you are pretty much *right, and have nothing left to learn about the one who made you and all that is?*

Most of us know the correct *biblical* answer to those questions, *but do our hearts betray us?* Do we in the depths of our soul question, accuse, and even insult God when we cannot understand what is going on?

Elihu would instruct us, and I believe Job would second this truth, that we should adopt this attitude as long as God gives us the strength to do so:

Always trust that God is with you, and trust that He is always right in his actions.

It is absolutely okay to be struggling and cry out to God, "I don't understand why this happening." But if we have the strength, we should also add, "But I will hold on to you, Father, because you are Holy and righteous!"

And of course, it is critical to invoke one of the most beautiful prayers in the Bible in such times. It was the prayer of a sinful pagan woman whose child was being tortured by a demon. It is all that needs to be said:

Lord, help me![146]

This lady saw in Jesus the light of life. It illuminated her sins, she had nothing to offer in return for the help she needed. She went with it - *Help me!*

Job was stripped bare of all his possessions, respect, and power. It came down to a moment where there was nothing but God and his naked, inadequate self.

It was wonderous, awesome, and entirely enough. Job's perspective on God and life was forever changed.

The light of life penetrated to his spirit.

Elihu's Directive on Handling Tough Times

The first few principles of Elihu in handling the challenges of life might be summarized as follows:

> *In moments of confusion, pain, and doubt as we struggle to walk side-by-side with our Father, if we can just trust his heart and know that his purposes are good and that we will be blessed with light – we can perhaps honor our Creator as he deserves.*

As we learned from the conversation between God and Job, even if we are not able to succeed at this in our human weakness, things are still good. If you are a child of God, you are in the unfailing grip of our merciful and gracious God. We should memorize the words of the Lord delivered through Isaiah:

Who is this...marching in the greatness of his strength? It is I, speaking in righteousness, mighty to save.[147]

It is so true that at times life gives us more trouble than we can process as individuals. We will not always deal with our challenges as well as we would hope, but then that is one of the great messages of Job's story – *God is the hero, not us.*

But if we can meditate on this lesson that Elihu shares, perhaps we can respond better in the future than we have in the past when things are challenging. Perhaps if we do *train like we fight,* and we brace ourselves mentally to always endeavor to *trust God's heart and lean not on our own understanding,*[148] *we may in the future respond with greater faithfulness.* If we do, we will benefit from the whole ugly experience that Job and his friends went through.

The initially unnamed one, Elihu, got a lot right about God and Job's situation. But we are not done with Elihu's words yet.

CHAPTER 9

ALWAYS DEFEND GOD

I volunteer at a summer camp every year. It is sponsored by a number of area churches. I am told the camp is *rustic,* which I have decided is probably a Latin word for *filthy* or *uncomfortable.*

This past year, I was awakened at 1:30 in the morning by a rather large hulking man – a bit scary at first. But then I heard the voice, it was my close friend Brady, a young counselor at the camp.

Hey, Mister Steve, I've got someone who is asking questions about God I can't answer – can you come help?

This is the way camp works. Some of the deepest issues come up in the middle of the night. I got up, put on some shorts and a t-shirt and went to meet the questioner. It turned out to be a teenager I was very familiar with. I'll call him Andy, but he and I had known each other for a while and he was a good guy.

I sat down, "What's on your heart Andy?"

"I just don't know if I can follow a God who would condemn tribes in Africa who have never heard of him to hell," Andy shared.

"What's are the names of the names of these tribes?" I queried.

"Hmm, what?" he replied.

"I mean which tribes are they, what cities are they near or in, and how do you know that no one has ever gone to them with the good news?" I continued.

"Well, they're out there, I don't know where," he stated, sounding less confident now.

This is a fairly common objection to the God of the Bible. I knew he had no tribal names or locations, it is an entirely theoretical objection. But at the heart of it is the same contention that Job made in so many ways, that being that *God is unjust to the core of his being.*

I had similar objections when I was Andy's age. My questions to Andy were designed to show the one who would accuse God of being an unreasonable tyrant that their objections are not well founded. In fact, their objections are made in utter ignorance. The real problem behind these accusations against God is too high an estimation of one's own intelligence and a despicably low and inaccurate view of God. I continued the conversation by bringing in some other Bible stories that showed that those who knew God best *insisted and trusted that God was justice personified.*

I have a rather cynical sense of sarcasm that the Holy Spirit mostly gives me the strength to hold purely within me. On this night, fortunately, he gave me that strength. What I thought of as this young man hurled his accusations against the loving and just Father who created us both was; *who are you to question the One True God that you don't even know, you little snot-nosed punk?*

It is harsh, but it is *true.* It is not an insult to Andy, it is truly the question that could be asked – that gets to the heart of the situation. Don't take my word for it, let us listen as Elihu continues his defense of the goodness and justice of the Almighty.

Job's Words Come Back on Him

In Chapter 34, Elihu begins his defense of the justice of God by first saying back to Job the accusations he had made against his Creator. While we have already made the case that Job was way out of line, in some ways I think Elihu shares my blunt sense of sarcasm:

> *For Job has said, 'I am in the right, and God has taken away my right; in spite of my right I am counted a liar; my wound is incurable, though I am without transgression.' What man is like Job who drinks up scoffing like water, who travels in company with evildoers and walks with wicked men? For he has said, 'It profits a man nothing that he should take delight in God.'*[149]

Whew, how did that sound to Job in that moment? Was he already cringing at what he had said, or was he still firmly holding to his perceived self-righteousness? The first part of what Elihu is saying, about being *right,* is not an actual quote. Elihu just took all of what Job had said and made a statement that sounds rather *sarcastic* but is actually very accurate.

Elihu had much the same response to Job that I had with Andy – except that Elihu let the words out. It is remarkable, that although it is likely that Elihu admired Job greatly from who he had been in his life prior to this tragedy – when the man he admired insulted *his God,* he crossed a line that Elihu was willing to fight over. He would risk the relationship with Job entirely in order to defend the God that he knew!

In Elihu's heart, speaking poorly of God was *never to go unopposed, even if defending God cost you much!* It is a powerful reminder of the zealous love of youth, much as the young shepherd boy David had.

David was the runt of the litter, apparently, in his family. He was younger, perhaps not as handsome, and was assigned to the menial child-labor task of watching the sheep. One day his father Jesse has another not-so-vital task for young David – to take some food to his three older brothers who were fighting in King Saul's army.

David heads to the battle and arrives, finds his brothers, and just as he is greeting them the giant warrior known as Goliath comes out and taunts the forces of Saul. He hurls curses and challenges their way – and everyone, including King Saul, is terrified. Except on this day, the young lunch bag delivery boy is there, and when he hears the words of the giant, he is furious:

Who is this uncircumcised Philistine, that he should defy the armies of the living God?[150]

Now David had faced some challenges as a young man. His dad's sheep had been attacked by a lion once, and also by a bear. David *killed them!* He chased these animals that had taken a sheep from the flock, took the sheep out of their mouth, *and killed them!* That's impressive! He was good with a sling – he was likely young, small, and fast.

But he was no match in battle for the experienced victor that Goliath was. As King Saul told David when someone brought him in to see the King:

You are not able to against this Philistine and fight with him, for you are but a youth, and he has been a man of war from his youth.[151]

Saul was right, you know, from a human perspective. It is one thing to be a good shepherd boy, but combat is whole different matter. Managing the relationship between shield and sword is a complex skill David had no training or experience in. He was no match for the experienced and powerful warrior who stood taunting the whole army to come and fight.

But David believed two things:

1.   It is not right to insult or challenge God in any way.

2.   God will fight for us if we trust him and run toward the battle.

David's words to his King stir our hearts thousands of years later:

Your servant struck down both lions and bears, and this uncircumcised Philistine shall be like one of them, for he has defied the armies of the living God... The LORD who delivered me from the paw of the lion and the paw of the bear will deliver me from the hand of the Philistine.[152]

Do you see what is happening here? It isn't that David is just some overconfident, testosterone-fueled fool. He knows *how* he was able to kill lions and bears. It was the strength and *tactical* wisdom that his God supplied in the moment of need.

And he also knew, that *no one was going to insult his awesome God without a fight.*

Elihu feels the same way.

And here is a gut-check for us all. Do you defend the goodness of God with all of your being? Do you hold God in such high esteem that jokes about him make you uncomfortable? Do you listen to those raising questions about the justice of God and find yourself bristling internally at the thought? Do you use your words for God as mere exclamations in ordinary conversation? (i.e., OMG, or "Jesus Christ, I can't believe you did that?") Do your find yourself thinking, *who do you think you are to insult my Lord, you little snot-nosed punk?*

And for that manner, how do you think of God yourself? When things are tough, are you disappointed in your "self-help genie" for not coming through for you? Do you look at how he has made you and continually complain and find fault? Do you look at your life situation and blame God for failing you? Are you ashamed to bring up God to coworker or fellow student because you are afraid of repercussions or rejection?

David wasn't. He rejected Saul's armor,[153] choosing instead to wear his shepherd clothing and take his sling and a few stones into battle. But above all, *he took the LORD into battle*, or shall we say the LORD took him! He risked *all* to defend the absolute purity and goodness of God.

There will be some practical considerations about developing this kind of impassioned love of and defense of God at the end of this chapter, but for now, let us list this as one of the desirable attributes of Elihu and David – an irresistible need to defend God.

Elihu's View of the Majestic One

> *Far be it from God that he should do wickedness, and from the Almighty that he should do wrong.*[154]

The God that Elihu *knew* was incapable of doing wrong. In his world, the Almighty and all of his attributes were *immutable* – the characteristic of *never* changing over time.

In other words:

- God *is* good, all the time.

- God *is* loving, all the time.

- God *is* just, all the time.

Does this square with your view of God? Job loved God through everything he did, but he believed, apparently, that God could make a mistake. This possibility seems to have been drawn from Job's own very high estimation of his own righteousness, combined with his belief that when bad things happened to people, that God was punishing them.

Notice, though, that Elihu likely struggled with this same belief:

He repays people according to their deeds. He treats people as they deserve.[155]

This is an important lesson to draw from this story as well; Elihu gets a lot of things right; he is the only one of the 5 men in the story who is *not* rebuked by God. But contrary to what Elihu has stated, Job *is not being treated as he deserves!* Elihu is right that God cannot do wrong; but he is wrong in this assessment of why Job is suffering. Job is suffering *because he is God's child.* He is caught in the battle between God and the rebellious Satan.

The lesson from this *mistake* of Elihu is this; when dealing with the knowledge of the Almighty, we should be humble. As Job mentioned in the final chapter of the story, there is a great difference between knowing about God versus *experiencing him and realizing how much there is to know!*

But to cement something good about Elihu's view, adopting the mindset that God's character is *immutable* can help each of us so much. If we devote time and meditation to the character of God, we can better *sort* through our challenges. When we have the unchanging nature of God firmly in our hearts and minds, and we fully embrace that our Creator is always just, loving, compassionate, gracious, merciful, and can be nothing else – it helps us to recognize who is speaking when our thoughts turn to the possibility that God is being cruel or unfair.

Those accusatory words that make us consider that God is suddenly unfair or in error are the words of Satan. The more fully we *learn the attributes of God, the less likely we are to misinterpret what is happening to us.* More fully coming to know the Almighty *requires* that we spend regular (daily) time in his Word, meditating, listening, and speaking to him. We can grow in our knowledge of our Father through reading what other believers have shared through books, and through being a member of God's family in a local church. We must continually nurture our relationship with and knowledge of the Holy One.

Elihu was not perfect, but *he was impressively strong for someone who was young!* No details are given as to how he nurtured his faith – but his faith is *substantial*, and his view of the *immutable* God is strong. We should endeavor to develop the same.

It All Falls Apart Without God

Questions are often a great way to begin to take apart a bad idea.

Elihu has a great question:

Did someone else put the world in his care? Who set the whole world in place?

He's on to something. So often we hear someone objecting to God because of "all the evil in the world." But as many thinking people have pointed out, *evil* is *only* evil if there is a standard of what *is* good.

If the world had formed completely by accident by natural forces, what would be the standard of evil? We do not recoil in horror when a lion chases down a baby gazelle and slaughters it. We do not protest and demand that the government make such actions illegal. We understand that animals behave like animals – we would expect nothing less.

But when someone intentionally harms a child, by physical, sexual, or emotional abuse – we suddenly are deeply moved with one thought – *it is wrong to harm a child.*

Both creatures are *small.* Both cannot defend themselves. Why is one so wrong, and the other not?

The human child is made in the image of her God. She is precious, and we recognize that from deep within the core of our being – because we too are made in the image of God! It offends us *because* the abuse or harm of a precious child *offends him!* It is wrong to treat something with such inestimable value and beauty with anything other than tender loving care.

Elihu's point is this: The world and all that is in it belongs to God. That includes each one of us. We are his.

He allows us freedom, even the freedom to rebel against him. And there is an eternal punishment for those that do – if they do not repent and return to the tender care of their Creator. He wants to save us all, but he wants our love. He could give us no choice, but that would be unloving of him. We would be captives.

He wants *lovers.*

The nature of the world tells us that God is awesome. He enjoys creating things of beauty. He loves his children. He loves us so much that he gives us the freedom to choose not to follow him – but he will pursue us to reclaim us.

In the end, all of humanity, past and present, will appear before the righteous Judge and give an answer for what we did with the awesome opportunity to take part in this epic adventure of life. None of us voted to give him that position as the judge of all – it is his by virtue of his perfect and eternal existence that *he reigns*.

None of us has the legal standing to object. In actuality, none of us should even dream of *questioning his goodness, or his motives.* But as we learned with Job, our Creator and Judge understands our weakness, and he shows us unmerited favor if we are in him.

As an application of this, it would be very wise for each of us to *abide* in the Word and the person of our Creator in order to develop a growing and fuller understanding of Who God Is. He is the "I AM WHO I AM;"[156] dare we say we are his equal by questioning his actions?

The Jewish people of old were so respectful of the use of the Father's proper name that the pronunciation of it is now uncertain. The *transliteration* of it for years was Jehovah, but it the word YHWH. Some have suggested that it is the sound we make when we breath. But any name we use for God should be uttered with fearful respect. *We should live and breathe praise for our Maker!* He is that awesome and beautiful. We should never use any descriptor for God as a swear word or thoughtless expression of amazement. No OMG! The casual passing of words that convey our idea of our Creator or Savior across our lips are an indication of a lack of understanding of the I AM WHO I AM.

We Exist at His Pleasure

If God were to take back his spirit and withdraw his breath, all life would cease, and humanity would turn again to dust.[157]

Once again, I perceive that one of the reasons Elihu was so infuriated with Job was because *he dared to insult the Almighty.* Although he no more understood the reason why Job was suffering than Job himself did, he was *undone* by Job's contention that *his life would be better if God would leave him alone!*[158] He was angered that Job contended that *God was his enemy!*[159]

Elihu's rebuke is something we all need to think of daily. *If God were to leave us alone, we would be dead!* He is the author, designer, builder, grantor, and guarantee of each breath we take.

A world without God is *death*. There have been ideas tried in the society of men that demonstrate this. The popular song *Imagine* by the late John Lennon stirred many hearts – it insinuated that life without heaven (i.e., without God) and "no religion too" would solve the problems of mankind.

The problem is the ideas presented by Lennon have been tried *repeatedly*. A group of French socialists set out to write a history of the glories of socialism, an ideology which enshrines the *reason* of man (i.e., the absence of God), and instead wrote a scathing condemnation of its repeated results. They noted that more than 100 million people were murdered by their own governments in the 20th century alone.[160] There is no need to *imagine* a world without God; far from what Lennon contended, the results are *hell.*

Elihu was right in his rebuke of Job's musings about life without God being better. Life without God is unimaginably horrible.

Remember that.

When All Else Fails – God is Awesome

I have to stress this. Although Elihu is remarkable – he is not perfect in his understanding. He is also, like Job, not the hero of this intense drama presented in the Bible.

But after four chapters of challenging Job's assumptions, and not necessarily being right in all of his assertions – he does something that is always right.

He knows he has already said a whole lot of words. And so he begs for some patience from his listeners, especially the one covered in boils from his head to his feet:

Bear with me a little, and I will show you, for I have yet something to say on God's behalf...[161]

Elihu is really wound up now. As much as he wanted to deal with the heresy he heard from Job, he is just now getting to the matter that burns within his heart the most.

> *I will get my knowledge from afar and ascribe righteousness to my Maker. For truly my words are not false; one who is perfect in knowledge is with you.*[162]

Scanning some of the books and commentaries from earlier days, many perceive that his *knowledge from afar* is the inspiration from the Holy Spirit of God. The Holy Spirit is first mentioned in the creation account found in Genesis. The Spirit very frequently is a *giver of words* when they are so badly needed. It seems to be likely here, that Elihu is not making a statement of out-of-control pride when he claims to be *perfect in knowledge,* he is merely letting Job and the friends know that he perceives what he is about to say as being received from God himself.

What he is about to unleash is unadulterated praise for the Lord of Hosts; it is similar to Mary's *Magnificat;*[163] her song of praise for what God was doing through her and for the world through her Holy Spirit pregnancy.

As such, let's take a look at the key points of Elihu's Magnificat, and determine what we should always keep in mind as we face the challenges of living for God every day.

God is Mighty, and does not Despise Any

We as creatures are often intimidated by people of power, and are contemptuous of others.

In the second gulf war, I was flying the Deputy Secretary of Defense, Paul Wolfowitz, around Iraq on a couple of occasions. He was *very* high up in my chain of command. He wielded a lot of power and influence over people such as me.

As we traveled together, there came a day he approached me and asked, "How are things going for you guys over here, Steve?" Just to be clear, we were not so familiar with each other that we were on a first name basis, he just read my name off of my name tag and was being friendly.

But I momentarily was cautious. I paused before I responded. I *knew* what I *should say!* "Oh, everything is wonderful sir, we are proud to be over here fighting for America, democracy, and apple pie!" But being first and foremost a child of the King of the universe, and having studied oaths and vows (such as the type of oath I had taken as a military officer), I also felt the gravity of the burden of being truthful to the question and my oath.

So I asked the Secretary an honest question: "Do you want the truth?"

He understood what I was asking, he replied, "No retribution, I want the truth."

And so we had a long talk. A few days later the Secretary went back to the States and started rattling cages over what I had told him. I was called to my commander's office and questioned – "What did you tell Wolfowitz?"

I replied, "I answered his question."

They continued, "But what did you tell him?"

I said, "I told him the truth."

I wish I had had a body camera on me. The look of absolute frustration and confusion on my commander's face was amusing. How do you say, "You shouldn't answer a question truthfully to the Deputy Secretary of Defense?"

But I was no hero. I was just trying to honor the God who gave me life and sustained me. I was trying not to be intimidated by human status.

And Elihu reminds us that our Lord has *no regard* for either the heights of human status nor the depths of poverty – we all stand before him in equality. He sees his creature made in his image, and as he noted on the sixth day of making the earth, he sees something *very good!*[164]

That. Is. Awesome.

When we see those who seem to be above the law – we should remember that it is simply not true. We should never mistake someone getting away with evil as a permanent status – we should remember the words of the Psalmist Asaph:

Truly God is good…to those whose hearts are pure. But as for me, I almost lost my footing...for I envied the proud when I saw them prosper despite their

wickedness. They seem to live such painless lives; their bodies are so healthy

and strong. They don't have troubles like other people; they're not plagued with

problems like everyone else...These fat cats have everything their hearts could

ever wish for! ...Look at these people – enjoying a life of ease while their riches

multiply...[165]

Asaph's words are very similar to Job's up to this point, Job had said this in reply to

Zophar earlier in the story:

Why do the wicked live, reach old age, and grow mighty in power? Their

offspring are established in their presence, and their descendants before their

eyes. Their houses are safe from fear, and no rod of God is upon them.[166]

Asaph and Job are struggling with something that so many of us do – we are wanting

to serve God but sometimes it seems we are just getting kicked in the teeth at every turn

while some of the most rebellious people we know are laughing at us from their yachts.

But by the time Asaph wrote this Psalm, he had done something to remind himself of

what the truth really is:

So I tried to understand why the wicked prosper. But what a difficult task it is!

Then I went into the sanctuary, O God, and I finally understood the destiny of the

wicked. Truly, you put them on a slippery path and send them sliding over the cliff

of destruction. In an instant they are destroyed, completely swept away by terrors.

When you arise, O Lord, you will laugh at their silly ideas as a person laughs at

dreams in the morning.[167]

When we are in the midst of confusion, thinking past the pain to the long-term realities can be very tough. Asaph had to put himself in the presence of God in order to break out of his negative funk. The *sanctuary of God* is available to us, if we will take advantage of it. When we are in pain and wanting relief – the tendency is to medicate. We eat, we get drunk, we take drugs, we have sex (real or virtual), or we use some other fantasy distraction. But Asaph ran to the shelter of the protective wings of God[168]. He asked for comfort and understanding from God.

Job found the same understanding when he was surrounded by the presence of God in the storm.

And what a comfort it is to know that our God does not regard the status of man. He is always righteous, and we should never mistake his patience with the wicked for approval of their choices. He wants them to *be* where we *are, under the same protective wings, wearing the beautiful robes of righteousness provided by the Christ.*

Elihu correctly describes truth – God does at times deal severely with the godless:

> *The godless in heart cherish anger; they do not cry for help when he binds them. They die in youth, and their life ends among cult prostitutes.*[169]

God does this in his wisdom, when he knows and sees a heart that is hardened beyond redemption. But then, God has also used *discipline* to correct godless people, such as when Nebuchadnezzar became too proud – and the Almighty struck him with madness.[170] When the pagan King's sanity returned, he stated something that sounded much like a statement of Elihu:

> *Now I, Nebuchadnezzar, praise and glorify and honor the King of heaven. All his acts are just and true, and he is able to humble the proud.*[171]

But then Elihu delivers a special message that is directed at Job:

> *By means of their suffering, he rescues those who suffer. For he gets their attention through adversity.*[172]

We have the backstory of Job's suffering. We are privy to the heavenly wager that led to the enormous losses he suffered. And we can see that although the affliction of Job for the purpose of the wager was indeed without reason – it would seem that God did have in mind a particular severe mercy for Job. God did indeed open Job's eyes through the adversity he endured, so that when God appeared, he could truly see his beauty alone.

Our God does not despise *anyone.* But perhaps we should use Peter's statement of this principle for clarity:

> *I see very clearly that God shows no favoritism.*[173]

God did not push this tragedy on Job because he was rich. Nor did he withhold suffering from Job because he was so valuable to the community. God sought the eternal best for Job, while also demonstrating his own holiness and Satan's absolute corruption.

There are several lessons we could learn from all of this, but one great comfort is this: if you are struggling to find meaning and make sense of what is happening in your life – you can know that God is seeking your best. In so doing, he will bring glory to himself. We would do well to remember the warning that Elihu delivers to Job in this moment:

> *Beware lest wrath entice you into scoffing.*[174]

If we do not have a firm grasp on the holiness and the immutable character of our Creator – the challenges that God allows to glorify him and to transform us more into his image may cause us to fall away and to bring shame upon his great name.

We must endeavor to more fully know our Lord every day.

The Leaping Heart

You must read this section of the story out loud. Elihu begins speaking in Job Chapter 32, but in Chapter 36 something begins to happen around them. Shortly after his admonishment to *extol God's work*[175] he begins speaking of how God:

> *...Draws up the drops of water, they distill his mist in rain, which the skies pour down...can anyone understand the spreading of the clouds, the thunderings of his pavilion?...He scatters his lightning about him...and commands it to strike its mark.*[176]

A storm is brewing, and as Elihu observes the power of the weather as God designed and ordained it, and as the wind and water drops begin to pelt him, he becomes lost in his excitement for the awesome power of the Almighty:

> *At this also my heart trembles and leaps out of its place...God thunders wondrously with his voice; he does great things that we cannot comprehend.*[177]

My wife and I produced four children. Like pretty much everyone, we sat through the schoolhouse explanations of how children are made. There's the sex, the sperm joining with the egg, the growth in the womb, and eventually the baby travels down the birth canal and emerges. It all makes sense, right?

Not at all. I've watched it and helped my wife through each of the four births – it is beyond comprehension. How does this tiny human get constructed through a combination of genetic instructions and food from its mother? The code in the DNA provided by the parents constructs a particular person, of a particular sex, with a unique personality – all starting (normally) with two people just enjoying each other physically.

How does that *really* happen? The complexity of the information required to provide the instructions to construct each child is mind-boggling!

Even a single functioning short-chain protein is very complex. It contains more than a hundred amino acids combined in a particular order, and proteins can accomplish different functions depending on that order. Dr. Stephen Meyer wrote the following on the problem with DNA:

> *Even taking the probabilistic resources of the whole universe into account, it is extremely unlikely that even a single protein of that length [the shortest protein length] would have arisen by chance on early earth.*[178]

Notice he is not even speaking of DNA and its volumes of information that construct a human (or other creature); just a comparatively simpler building block of life. Not only does DNA have the coding for what a baby human is to be, it *directs* the construction through biological processes. Humans are *self-replicating,* a totally amazing concept when you think of it. While we humans have built some amazing computers, cars, airplanes, machines, and other devices – imagine if these machines were self-replicating. What if a few years after you brought a new car, you came out to your garage and another new car had been replicated from within your trusty machine during the night?

Can you imagine the complexity of the code and machinery required to have a functioning car that can also reproduce another car while still functioning every day? Sexual reproduction is beyond complex – while we know much about it, we can't seem to even come close to the technologically amazing process of a woman and man enjoying an evening of togetherness, joining some basic information bearing components together in the woman's womb, and then the replication of human baby takes place over the next nine months as she goes on about her business. *He does great things we cannot comprehend.*[179]

It is a sort of *everyday miracle* – we are so used to it and yet, each time I watched the birth process, it brought me to tears. *How does that happen?*

Elihu is observant, much as the writer of the Proverbs was. They both looked around and critically thought through what they were observing – and marveled. In Proverbs the observer notes:

> *There are three things that amaze me – no, four things that I don't understand: how an eagle glides through the sky, how a snake slithers on a rock, how a ship navigates the ocean, how a man loves a woman.*[180]

Once again, this writer is speaking of things we see every single routine boring day of our lives in some cases. But these things when studied and pondered – are amazing. We can talk a lot about the mechanics of such actions, we have learned much about *some* of it. But the fact that self-replicating creatures such as an eagle, can not only apply the mechanics of flight, *but that they are constructed through genetic information to masterfully exist in the air is astounding.* The complexity of the software language required for an eagle to simultaneous manipulate its muscles to conduct a high-speed dive on a prey and pull out at just the right moment to break the neck of its next meal without breaking its own body is, well, incomprehensible.

Every day, if we are observant, we can see things beyond comprehension all around us. It is the signature of our Creator. At a certain point in Elihu's rapturous praise, he stops and focuses on the boil-covered man:

Pay attention to this Job. Stop and consider the wonderful miracles of God![181]

This is great advice for any of us to help us keep our heads on straight. I learned this from my first daughter Rachel. My wife and I have always enjoyed hiking, and we would go to a park and hike the trails. I would be enjoying the sun, trees, wind, and cool temperatures. Rachel would suddenly stop, crouch down, and excitedly exclaim, "Look at this bug!" She had this ability to look at the details around us, and she would see the most amazing creatures and plants.

She is an adult now, but because of her youthful curiosity, whether in the woods or in a major downtown area, I am looking at the details. There are amazing things of beauty beyond comprehension all around. My first child gave me the gift of knowing what David had discovered:

The heavens proclaim the glory of God. The skies display his craftsmanship. Day after day they continue to speak; night after night they make him known They speak without a sound or word; their voice is never heard. Yet their message has gone throughout the earth, and their words to all the world.[182]

Elihu is enthralled with the work of his Creator. What he observes around him tells him so much about the Almighty he serves:

- He loves to create.

- He loves beauty.

-       He is awesome and beyond comprehension in power and understanding.

-       He can do things we cannot even begin to attempt *or conceive*.

And from this habit of careful observation of the testimony of the power of God through what he has made, he encourages Job to consider that God can *always* be trusted. He has the power to bring us through times that we *cannot* see through. His creation contains so many elements that we cannot fully comprehend, and we certainly cannot as mere mortals produce within our own strength. Yet his and Job's God can do these things as an *afterthought,* it would seem. They are easy and natural for the Creator of all things. He speaks and they are.

Interestingly, Elihu goes into a line of questioning that will soon be repeated by God himself in form. The basic line of thought of Elihu that is posed to Job goes like this:

-       Look at the incomprehensible and wondrous things God does easily.

-       Can you do them?

-       You cannot, so wouldn't it be wise to realize you have no standing to question God?

Elihu's Conclusion

We cannot look at the sun, for it shines brightly in the sky when the wind clears

away the clouds. So also, golden splendor comes from the mountain of God. He is

clothed in dazzling splendor. We cannot imagine the power of the Almighty; but

even though he is just and righteous, he does not destroy us. No wonder people

fear him. All who are wise show him reverence.[183]

Elihu is encouraging us all to develop a far more accurate vision of who God is.

When we have a small concept of God, we will have huge problems in life.

Job had perhaps made a bit of an idol out of himself, out of his own ability to do good. And he had brought God down just a few notches, to the level of a slightly exalted peer *human* who had made a grievous error against him.

Elihu admonishes Job, through his impassioned praise for the beautiful and awesome world the Creator had made, to reconsider *how he viewed God.* As he warns, *"no wonder people fear him,"*[184] he is making a statement repeated by those who had experienced God's glory throughout history. One of the psalmists wrote, "The fear of the LORD is the beginning of wisdom; all those who practice it have a good understanding."[185]

Surveying the various stories of those who have experienced the power of God, we see that *fear* is a natural and appropriate response to the awesomeness of who he is. Yet fear is not where God wants us to stay. One of the very common instructions of Jesus, who was fully God in the flesh, was, "Do not be afraid."[186] When we arrive in the presence of God for eternity, after the day of judgment, it will be amazing. We will then fully comprehend the *fear* of the awesomeness of who God is, and at the same time be enthralled with the consuming love of God.

We should strive, Elihu would contend, to see God more fully each day as he truly is.

Doing so will transform our estimation of our earthly problems, much as it did for the Apostle Paul:

> *So we do not lose heart. Though our outer self is wasting away, our inner self is being renewed day by day. For this light momentary affliction is preparing us for an eternal weight of glory beyond all comparison, as we look not to the things that are seen but to the things that are unseen. For the things that are seen are transient, but the things that are unseen are eternal.*[187]

CHAPTER 10

MEMORIALS

We have dealt extensively with the love of Elihu for his God. But he brings up one more challenge in his words that are very instructive:

> *Because of the multitude of oppressions people cry out; they call for help because of the arm of the mighty. But none says, 'Where is God my maker, who gives songs in the night, who teaches us more than the beast of the earth and makes us wiser than the birds of the heavens?*[188]

Life is hard. We have some really wonderful days and some times of peace, but probably all of us realize that it *will not last.* There will be a sad phone call, an accident, an immense natural disaster, or some other event that shatters our peace.

In those times, Elihu notes, people call out to God and ask for help.

But what about during those good times? Do we use our peaceful moments to recognize and build a monument of strength toward God in our hearts and minds? Do we collect those *songs in the night* and sing them back to God as a reminder of what he has done in our lives? Are we intentional in the creation of *memorials and disciplines* through which we can continually strengthen our faith for the rough times?

Or do we just wait until the crisis is upon us and *only then seek God's face?* Do we use God like a fire extinguisher, or are we being intentional in our walk with him? What would God recommend?

Twelve Stones

Israel, after 40 years of wandering in the desert due to their lack of trust in God, are finally moving toward the promised land. Moses has died. Joshua is now in command.

God is about to do something miraculous to show Israel that he is with Joshua just as he was working through Moses. The Jordan river must be crossed. But it is at flood stage, it was *overflowing its banks*[189] and was fast moving and dirty. Joshua leads Israel to the edge of the Jordan, the priests are leading the way, carrying the Ark of the Covenant on its poles. Joshua has told the people what will happen, that the LORD will dry up this raging river when they get to it.

As the priest move toward the Jordan and their feet touch the water, its flow rapidly dwindles to nothing. They continue into the very middle of the channel and stand while the whole nation of Israel passes through. Joshua picks up 12 stones and erects an altar to God while they are passing. Then the stones are taken with them, the priest walk to the other bank, and the river roars back into its place behind them.

Joshua sets up the 12 stones in the next place where they make camp, and tells of their purpose:

> When your children ask their fathers in times to come, "What do these stones mean?" then you shall let your children know, "Israel passed over this Jordan on dry ground." For the LORD your God dried up the waters of the Jordan for you until you passed over, as the LORD your God did to the Red Sea, which he dried up for us until we passed over...[190]

The LORD knows that we are forgetful people. He knows a present danger can overshadow a previous victory, and make us forget the previous provisions of God.

He should know – he made us!

And thus, throughout Scripture he institutes remembrances. The twelve stones had a particular purpose in the daily life of his people:

> ...*So that all the peoples of the earth may know that the hand of the LORD is mighty, that you may fear the LORD your God forever.*[191]

Because of our forgetfulness, because of the tyranny of the immediate threat, we need *memorials and disciplines* in our lives to strengthen the knowledge of what God has done in our life. We need to dwell on what we have seen his mighty hand do for us on *a regular basis,* so that when a challenge appears, the *fact of God's presence in our lives immediately looms large.*

When Israel first approaches the walled city of Jericho, it had to be an imposing threat. Israel's army had virtually no combat experience. Jericho was prepared for action, it wasn't their first rodeo. The plan handed down by God seemed, well, lackluster to say the least.

Israel's army was to approach the large and thick walls with bow wielding defenders perched on top and, wait for it, quietly walk around the city one time each day for six days.

Wow. That had to inspire some doubt on the part of this inexperienced army.

The seventh day they were to walk around the city seven times, trumpets would be blown, and then everyone would, well, *shout.*

From a human standpoint, it was a ridiculous plan. It wasn't a plan at all.

What if Jericho's army rushed out to meet them while they walked in silence? What if they just shot at them from the walls and eliminated them through attrition during the week? What would all of this accomplish to the strong walls of Jericho with its experienced army inside anyway?

But each day, as they left camp, they could see the twelve stones. Each represented one of the tribes of Israel, and reminded them that each of their tribes, every individual, had seen God dry up a river suddenly, and the whole nation walked through an impossible situation.

So every one of the seven days, the army walked past the stones on the way to Jericho. The plan made no sense, but neither does walking through the channel of the Jordan river with a whole nation during harvest time when the river is raging and past its banks.

The message of the memorial stones was this:

> *You do not have to understand the plan, just know that I (the Almighty) am with you as I was when you crossed the Jordan and I will take care of you. Do not be afraid, look at the stones, remember my power, and stand firm.*

Do you have memorials in your life to remind you of those times when God showed up? Do you sing the songs that God has given you, those songs that have great meaning between you and him?

There are two songs I sing to God regularly. One is the old hymn, *When I Survey the Wondrous Cross.* I find that song brings to memory the true meaning of the cross, and of what Jesus did for me there. Read this, or better yet, *sing this to God* – think of what God has done for you:

> When I survey the wondrous cross
>
> On which the Prince of glory died,
>
> My richest gain I count but loss,
>
> And pour contempt on all my pride.
>
>
> Forbid it, Lord, that I should boast,
>
> Save in the death of Christ my Lord!
>
> All the vain things that charm me most,
>
> I sacrifice them to his blood.
>
>
> See from his head, his hands, his feet,
>
> Sorrow and love flow mingled down!
>
> Did e'er such love and sorrow meet,
>
> Or thorns compose so rich a crown?
>
>
> Were the whole realm of nature mine,
>
> That were a present far too small;

Love so amazing, so divine,

Demands my soul, my life, my all.[192]

This song, sung quietly to God, reminds me of the great love he has poured out upon me and all of his people. It also connects me with the millions of other believers who have sung this beautiful hymn to God since Isaac Watts first penned it over 300 years ago. I sense the presence of this amazing crowd of people, many of whom sung this in the dark when they were scared, lonely, and unsure of what to do next. And they were reminded to stand strong and trust that the Lord was going to take care of them.

Singing is such a blessing from God. As Elihu notes, it is something God has placed within us, for he is the originator of music. A singing memorial can be a powerful way to drive the truth that God is *always faithful* into our hearts.

Remember to Extol

> *Remember to extol his work, of which men have sung. All mankind has looked upon it; man beholds it from afar. Behold, God is great, and we know him not; the number of his years are unsearchable.*[193]

How do you make this instruction from Elihu to Job real in your life? What other ways can you regularly remember the work of your Creator in your life?

In my church we have been doing a purity mentoring program amongst us men. It is based on the *Conquer* video series by Dr. Ted Roberts[194]. One of his recommendations that really struck me as in keeping with Elihu's admonishments is to construct a survival kit. Roberts was a fighter pilot in the Vietnam era, and the survival kit went on every flight. It had essential items such as flares, radio, signal mirror, and medical supplies to help a pilot who goes down behind enemy lines to fix any wounds and find his way back to safety.

Roberts suggested making a pouch or holder of some type that contained items that remind you of God's strength and faithfulness in your life. It might be pictures of your spouse and kids, or of a special time in your life when God's presence saved you from a bad situation. Or perhaps it is an artifact, such as a rock, or a piece of a car that you wrecked and survived. It can be anything that you can bring out in your quiet times and in the tough times to remind you of the great works of the Almighty in your life.

Do This In Remembrance of Me

In my church, we take the Lord's Supper or *communion* every Sunday. I'm so thankful for this. I don't know how many times I have been sitting in worship with my church family when those emblems of the body and blood of the Christ suddenly are passed to me, and I discover that my mind and heart are not even present. The words of Jesus come to me:

This is my body, which given for you. Do this in remembrance of me.[195]

This is a memorial instituted by *Yeshua* himself! He knows my heart, and yours! We are so easily consumed by the worries of our life. We can be singing our hearts out about how great our God is while we are planning the workweek ahead. But then comes the memorial – Paul's words also come to me in moments such as these, when he was writing about this very special time of remembering:

> *Whoever, therefore, eats the bread or drinks the cup of the Lord in an unworthy*
> *manner will be guilty concerning the body and blood of the Lord. Let a person*
> *examine himself, then, and so eat of the bread and drink of the cup. For anyone*

who eats and drinks without discerning the body eats and drinks judgment on himself. That is why many of you are weak and ill, and some have died.[196]

Those are some powerful words! There have been times when some churches would hold what they called "closed communion" because of this verse. This meant if you visited their church and you were not a member there, you could not take communion because they were afraid of you being condemned by God for taking it in a wrong way.

But I do not see this to be warranted because of the way it is worded. It says each one should examine *themselves,* not that we should attempt to restrict or examine others for worthiness. Further, the words say not that God condemns us, but that we *drink judgment on ourselves.*

Paul does go on to say that we are *disciplined* by the Lord, and so he is certainly attentive to us in this time – for our good in his love. But isn't the condemnation just missing the opportunity and blessing of remembering that solemn, dreadful, and wonderful day when the Christ took our sins upon himself and conquered death? When we take the emblems of communion while distracted, we fail to receive the blessing of the strength that would be imparted if we really sought to think about Jesus' act of love on our behalf.

In other words, failing to remember while observing a memorial is an epic failure. We receive nothing of value if we do not see Christ and his atoning death and resurrection when we take of the emblems of the Lord's Supper.

What fascinates me about this memorial, about taking communion, are the varying responses it produces in me at different times.

I grew up in a culture which emphasized the solemn sacrifice, the pain, and how we should be sad that this had to happen.

Indeed, sadness is appropriate at times.

But I have also found myself sitting there with tears of joy as I think how God choosing to do something so despised by world has worked such a great thing in the lives of his children. Jesus screams from the cross, "It is finished!"[197] And yes, praise God, it was! I have freedom from that cry, and by his wounds I have been healed![198] Such joy is to be found when the Son of God did what only God could do.

And then lately, as I have refocused my heart and mind as the Lord's Supper is passed to, I have found myself full of wonder and confusion. I have recently prayed, "Lord, I don't even begin to understand this, it is too much for me."

Paul again states the wonder of what Jesus did so well:

> *For one will scarcely die for a righteous person – though perhaps for a good person one would dare even to die – but God shows his love for us in that while we were still sinners, Christ died for us. Since, therefore, we have now been justified by his blood, much more shall we be saved by him from the wrath of God. For if while we were enemies we were reconciled to God by the death of his Son, much more, now that we have ben reconciled, shall we be saved by his life. More than that, we also rejoice in God through our Lord Jesus Christ, through whom we now have received reconciliation.[199]*

That phrase, "while we were still sinners,"[200] it hits Paul hard. He once *persecuted* the followers of Jesus. Yet he, as he wrote this, was reminded that Jesus died for *him* not because he was worthy, but fully in the face of the truth that he was not!

And that is something I share with Paul. I was in complete rebellion to God as young adult. I denied his existence. I looked at the marvelous, complex, and beautiful world and gave the credit to *chance.* In short, I was an arrogant, rebellious, sinful, and utterly worthless moron.

Yet, *while I was still a moron,* Jesus did what he did because my Creator wanted me close.

And thus as the bread and the fruit of the vine come around now, I find myself, well, *astonished at the love and justice and mercy and compassionate grace of God!* I wish I could say to him, "Oh yeah, I see and understand why you did that!"

But I do not.

I am blown away that he did what he did. I am thankful to the core of my being that he did what he did.

But, I cannot comprehend it.

I sit in stunned amazement.

I remember with tears of joy, confusion, and awe.

Thank you, Yeshua, for that remembrance!

Memorials are powerful tools in building and maintaining our faith.

Train for War in Peacetime

What I take away from Elihu's various admonishments to remember is this – if I am to be strong in the time of testing, I must prepare *now.* I must make time with God in his presence, in his word, with his people, and with memorials – an inviolate priority.

It is so comforting to know that God forgave Job, Eliphaz, Bildad, Zophar, and even Stephen Moore their very great sins they chose when the pressure was on.

But I would so like to stand firm and praise God in the next challenge.

Choose your memorials, and remember to extol the great things the Almighty has done!

CHAPTER 11

WHAT FRIENDS DO

Eliphaz, Bildad, and Zophar. These were some of Job's closest friends. In all fairness, I think these friends of Job have been heaped with enough condemnation over the years. In all honesty, they do some things that are very noteworthy and good.

But I also perceive, if we could have them visit us, they would share some, "don't do this" kind of tips with us from their experience of the Almighty God that day as they sat with Job. Let's look at some lessons we can learn to help us better support people as they go through the challenges of life.

Be There

> *When three of Job's friends heard of the tragedy he had suffered, they go together and traveled from their homes to comfort and console him.*[201]

Do you ever dread going to the hospital, home, or funeral of someone close to you? I know I have. I've been to the funeral of my friend Terry (mentioned earlier) where there were three caskets from one family, while the two survivors sat wearing casts and back braces and sat in wheelchairs. I've been to a funeral of a father and being buried by his two sons. I've headed to the hospital of someone who had no hope of living and *knew it.*

Each time, there was dread and fear in my heart. What do I say? How do I respond if they ask, "Why did God let this happen?"

But then something Eliphaz, Bildad, and Zophar taught me many years ago has overridden my fear. Because of my love for those involved, I *just go*. My loving obligation is to just be there, and if appropriate (and led by the Holy Spirit) say nothing at all.

The three friends of Job heard of the horrendous losses and poor health of their friend – and they knew they must *go*. They arrived together and cried when they saw him. They tore their clothing in grief and covered themselves in dust. They identified with the suffering of their friend; they were *astonished* at the suffering of their friend.

And they sat down and were quiet.

> *Then they sat on the ground for seven days and nights. No one said a word to Job, for they saw that his suffering was too great for words.*[202]

Seven days, no words.

That *says* a lot.

It says that we are suffering with you, and we realize that no words can even begin to soothe the pain of the suffering at this point.

Calling Terry

It took me awhile but I called the friend I had mentioned in an earlier chapter who lost his wife and two of his three children in a car wreck. I knew I needed to call, but for so long I just wasn't sure what to say. I wanted to check up on my dear friend and just let him know that he was on my heart.

But I still, three months after the tragedy, had nothing to say to comfort my friend.

But remembering the example of Job's friends, I just decided to call and *be there* on the other end of the phone.

As we began to talk, I just confessed why I had not called earlier – I just did not know what to say. He understood, "There is nothing to be said. I'm just glad you called." We shared tears, confusion - we had no answers. I gave no wise words of comfort. But yet before we said our goodbye, he told me he *was comforted.*

For a few moments of his lonely day, someone was there with him in his grief.

When people we care about are suffering, we should not take counsel of our fears. What should we say if they ask why God allowed this? How about, "I don't have a clue." And then cry with them. Shut your pie hole and cry.

What Eliphaz, Bildad, and Zophar did for Job for seven days was beautiful, compassionate, empathic, caring, and very much needed. They silently represented the love of God for someone as his heart tried to take in what was beyond comprehension.

When people are hurting, confused, or even dying – just be there.

Listen

A truly wise person uses few words; a person with understanding is even-

tempered. Even fools are thought to be wise when they keep silent; with their mouths shut, they seem intelligent.[203]

This perhaps is a greater challenge today than it ever was in the past. The internet, web cams, going "live" on social media, having your own blog, or self-publishing a book — these avenues of a public platform are more readily available to just about anyone today than ever before. There is no requirement to be educated, demonstrate wisdom, or even have proper credentials — if you have a *smartphone,* you can shout your words to the world.

And so, we have become accustomed to saying much, but listening poorly.

And also, with the continual addictive nature of social media we also have failed to develop our minds. Most of us have never been trained, nor have we sought to be trained, how to think critically. We do not seriously study the Word of God. We lack wisdom.

Thus, our mouths tend to run while our ears are nearly deaf. We live in a time when *everyone talks continually, even when no one is truly listening.*

This is one thing the friends of Job do not do well. Job, quite frankly, is processing what has happened. He is hurt, angry, off-balanced, and otherwise completely undone.

And we can certainly understand that.

When he begins to speak and starts to question the justice of God, his friends *do not allow him to work through these feelings and just share what he is thinking inside.*

Instead, they hear what they strongly believe is an error in his thoughts (it is), and they *know* that they *know* what the problem is (they are badly mistaken)!

In fact, if you look at the motives of their advice, they actually believe that what they are telling him *will help to end his suffering!* They are fully convicted that they are right, and if Job will just listen to them and do what they say, everything will be better.

They are completely wrong.

It is strongly evident that Bildad, Eliphaz, and Zophar are fully convicted that they are seeking Job's best interest, but what hurtful and wrong things they say! Let's look at a few of these choice "truths" they share with their pathetic broken friend:

> *- Stop and think! Do the innocent die? When have the upright been destroyed? My experience shows that those who plant trouble and cultivate evil will harvest the same. A breath from God destroys them. They vanish in a blast of his anger.*

This is *horrible.* Job had just finished his first mournful words in seven days, and Eliphaz quickly begins *accusations!* He is saying that in his understanding of God's ways, good people are blessed by God, and evil people suffer punishment. Eliphaz fully believes this, convinced that Job has done something badly wrong – and that is exactly why Job has suffered such a punishment from God.

But that is not all – do you catch the fairly clear *implied* reason why Job's children died? When God is angry with evil people, a *breath from God* takes them out. His *blast of anger,* in other words, the great wind that brought the house down upon Job's ten children, is nothing less than what they deserved for their great evil – it is just the way God works!

Bildad punches Job in the gut a few minutes later:

Your children must have sinned against him, so their punishment was well deserved.[204]

As if that were not enough, Zophar drives one final nail into Job's hurting heart:

Listen! God is doubtless punishing you far less than you deserve![205]

All of these words taken together are shockingly cruel to Job and constitute blasphemy against God's character. But then we know a lot more of the story than Job or his friends did. They were all searching for reasons for Job's tragedy and ways to remedy it. We know that Job is wrong, God did not wrongly do anything to him – Job was suffering because that is what happens at times in the great war between God and Satan.

We know that the friends are wrong also, very wrong. Job is not guilty of some sin, nor is God being punitive. Job's children were casualties of war, not recipients of God's righteous anger.

Let's think this through. If you *were* one of Job's friends, and you found yourself feeling angry at his accusations against God, do you really think Job was ready to hear your advice?

Or would it have been more appropriate to be wise as Solomon recommended and just seek to be there, listen, and attempt to understand what your friend is struggling with? When a person is struggling with the process of grief, are we really sure they are ready for theological correction?

And for that manner, while we may be fully convinced that we know every aspect of God's character – do we really?

The friends of Job teach us wisdom.

It is right to be there.

It is right to be silent.

It is right to listen.

It is right to allow a grieving person to grieve and say things that we disagree with. If they are angry with God, the story of Job shows us clearly that *he can take it.* He's a big God, the only true God – and he loves his children, even when they are mistakenly frustrated with him.

Shut your pie hole, zip your lip. Restrain your words. Listen with your heart. Let people grieve fully and honestly.

The More Fully We Know God, The Humbler We Will Be

It is important to emphasize once again that the friends of Job fully believe they are doing what is best for Job – they *know* that he is suffering horribly *because he is guilty of some horrible sin against God.* For that matter, Job does not disagree, as we have pointed out in earlier chapters, that this is the nature of God as well! He just *knows* that God has made a mistake in singling him out for *punishment.* After all, Job is sure he is absolutely righteous!

None of these men seem to be spiritual slackers, their world centers around God. But their knowledge of *who they perceive God to be is not aligned with Who God actually is.*

Do we dare to be so bold as to think that we have the Almighty Lord of Host completely figured out?

In my informal surveys of the people I love dearly in my church, I have to admire one thing – their absolute honesty about their knowledge of Scripture and of God himself. My Bible class that meets on Sunday morning just pretty much 'fessed up a few years ago that they would rate themselves as *biblically illiterate!*

Honesty is a beautiful thing – but are we content to stay ignorant?

If we as followers of Christ have strong concepts of who God is and what is right and wrong in life, yet we are not daily seeking his face through his Word, are we not *cult members?* We believe what we have been told by Pastors, preachers, and other spiritual leaders – but we value time with God and his wisdom so little that we would rather entertain ourselves on an electronic device rather than seeking the Lord who gave us life. What does this say about our faith? What does it say about what we truly love?

The example of Job's friends in the context of today's non-reading believers should be a severe warning to us – as bad as Eliphaz, Bildad, and Zophar abused truth, we are far more likely to do far worse!

In our desires to comfort and help those we love as they go through the trials of life, we need to be there, listen, and be humble.

But to truly be an instrument of the Holy One, we must earnestly endeavor to continually draw near to him in order to better hear the voice of the Holy Spirit.

The Holy Spirit is one of the most commonly used *excuses* for slothful and careless faith in America today. When someone admonishes us to be *in the Word,* some believers claim that they are *Spirit-led* to justify their neglect of God himself.

The problem with being Spirit-led and hearing leading from him without *knowing the Word of God intimately* is that the Holy Spirit is not the only spirit-being out there! Satan and his demons are also spiritual beings, and if we do not know what God has said, we can be easily deceived at the *urges* and *still-small voices* we may hear.

We may be *demonic spirit-led!*

The *Spirit-led* believer who does not seriously listen to God through the inspired Word, by regular study, meditation, and prayer, is like the people God described through the prophet Isaiah:

> *...These people draw near with their mouth and honor me with their lips, while their hearts are far from me, and their fear of me is a commandment taught by men...*[206]

If we are not craving and continually dwelling in the inspired Word of God, we will not grow toward maturity. Claiming to be *Spirit-led* while being biblically illiterate is a logical contradiction. The lack of a priority in life to spend substantial time with our Lord in his Word is indicative of a heart problem.

Job's friends were fully convicted that they were spiritually wise, right, and being helpful – and yet they were completely in error. Or as God put it:

> *My anger burns against you and against your two friends, for you have not spoken what of me what is right...*[207]

Ask God to teach you humility.

And if you have proudly claimed to be a *Spirit-led believer* but know little of God's Word, repent and get serious about your relationship with God. We will talk about *how* to do that in the Epilogue.

CHAPTER 12

THE STORY OF JOB IS ABOUT

We have seen that there is so much more to the biblical story of Job than just the traditional handle placed on the book of *the problem of suffering.*

What intrigued me over the years as I continued to be fascinated by the story and kept studying and teaching it was that I referred to it often when speaking with others about God and spiritual challenges of any sort.

There just a lot of relevant truth in the story of the cosmic wager that applies to everyday life. We can strengthen our walk of faith by more fully understanding this ancient account of a man caught up in the battle between good and evil. For that battle still rages around us every day.

With that in mind, in this final chapter let us recap just a few of the more important faith lessons we have gleaned from the story and some possible daily applications. The story of Job is about the following.

1.   **Our View of God**

Job, Job's wife, Eliphaz, Bildad, Zophar and Satan all had something curiously in common – their view of the Almighty was distorted. As impressive as Job's holiness and service to his Creator was, we see his awe when he encounters the One he had followed for so long:

I had heard of you...but now my eye sees you; therefore I despise myself and repent...[208]

The words of A.W. Tozer are so appropriate here:

> *Among the sins to which the human heart is prone, hardly any other is more hateful to God than idolatry, for idolatry is at bottom a libel on His character. The idolatrous heart assumes that God is other than he is – in itself a monstrous sin – and substitutes for the true God one made in its own likeness. Always this God will conform to the image of the one who created it and will be base or pure, cruel or kind, according to the moral state of mind from which it emerges...the idolater simply imagines things about God and acts as if they were true.*[209]

Each of the primary characters, none of them spiritual slackers, had constructed an idol representing God in their hearts, and was living their lives within that view of God. As a result:

- Satan thought God would cast Job away if he cursed.

- Job thought his children's salvation hung by a thread.

- Job's friends *knew* Job had sinned and that was why God was punishing him.

  - Job's wife thought she knew how her husband could end his suffering.

  They were all *dead wrong* about God.

Yet with the exception of Satan, they were all dedicated and fairly mature believers in the Almighty. But Job ended up cursing God because of his erroneous view. Job's friends ended up hurting the friend they were trying to comfort because of their idolatry. And Job's wife, well, I'll give her a Mulligan on this one – I get why she said what she said. And so did God.

Elihu is interesting. As was mentioned, some of his statements seem to be holding much the same views as the others, but then again not. We perceive that he held in his heart a certain view of God, one that we would do very well to adopt. Although he seems uncertain as to why Job is suffering, he is certain that God is always *good.* He is sure that the heavenly Father always listens and responds, even if we cannot or will not hear. He *chooses* to side with and defend God. This attitude of firmness toward the immutable goodness of God is reminiscent of what one of the psalmists proclaimed:

> *Bless the Lord, O my soul! O LORD my God, you are very great! You are clothed with splendor and majesty, covering yourself with light as with a garment, stretching out the heavens like a tent...may the glory of the LORD endure forever; may the LORD rejoice in his works, who looks on the earth and it trembles, who touches the mountains and they smoke! I will sing to the LORD as long as I live; I*

will sing praise to my God while I have being. May my meditation be pleasing to him, for I rejoice in the LORD.[210]

How do we develop the attitude of Elihu and the psalmist?

You may not like the answer to this – you may have to change the way you live your life.

Your life will have to be *transformed* by God as a result of the difficult choice you must make in your life.

Will you continue, if you are the average western believer, to go with what is normal in society, even within our *Christian* society? Will you be a person who has strong beliefs about God and what he wants, attend church, and spend virtually no time listening to the Almighty through the inspired Word? Will you choose to get your spiritual knowledge from a pastor, talented speaker, or online video rather than sit with God daily and seek him through the written Word?

You see, the Bible that we have is the Bible that our heavenly Father made sure we would have. He guided believers like us through the centuries to ensure that the letters, histories, wisdom, and poetry that constitutes our modern Bible would be preserved accurately and completely – because he knew what we would need to hear from him.

The story of Job is one of those vital stories that *he* wanted us to deeply dive into in his presence – because he knows how easily we can construct an idol of him in our heart. The idol we construct in our ignorance, much as Job's and all of the characters of the story we have considered, is always *way too human*.

God isn't angry because we tend to do this, he understands very well and wants to help us in pursuing a higher (and more realistic) view of him. It was *the Lord himself* who moved those believers in the past to preserve, translate, and pass on the treasure that is Scripture – so that we could avoid the mistakes that we as mortal – spiritual creatures are so prone to.

As the Apostle Paul noted regarding the purpose of the writings of old:

> *For whatever was written in former days was written for our instruction, that through endurance and through the encouragement of the Scriptures we might have hope.*[211]

The problem that so many of us, especially in the United States, need to deal with is this: We *are biblically illiterate.*

We spend our time on social media, watch videos, listen to preachers/pastors/priest, and watch television.

We *do not listen* to God nor pursue his wisdom. We listen most effectively when we read the written word.

We. Do. Not. Read.

We. Do. Not. Listen.

Listening occurs when we sit down in a quiet place, intentionally, and we drink deeply of the whole Word of God. We come before him, praising him and begging him to teach us as we read from the sacred, God-breathed text. We ask God to change our hearts and minds as we do so. It is *vital* to realize that if we are to develop a more accurate view of our awesome God that we must use our *minds,* as Jesus the Christ so clearly spoke:

> *...You shall love the Lord your God with all your heart and with all your soul and* **with all your mind** *and with all your strength.*[212]

In our times, we are in love with love. But it is a very strange and shallow love we are embracing. It is based upon emotions and things *that stir our imagination* – not an enduring love based upon *the use of the mind* as Jesus commends above.

Note also, Jesus is *not* actually saying anything new, but rather just repeating a command from the Old Law given to Israel. This is the wisdom from God from long ago – yet why in our age are we so far from loving God *with our mind?* Author J.P. Moreland laments:

> *While few would actually put it in these terms, faith is now understood as a blind act of will, a decision to believe something that is either independent of reason or that is a simple choice to believe while ignoring the paltry lack of evidence for what is believed. By contrast with this modern misunderstanding, biblically, faith is a power or skill to act in accordance with the nature of the kingdom of God, a trust in what we have reason to believe is true. Understood in this way, we see that faith is built on reason.*[213]

Given our society's modern emphasis on *feelings-based belief,* and the concurrent idea of relativism – can you perceive the danger of an American believer having very erroneous and inaccurate conceptions of God?

Here's the truth in the form of a challenge to each person reading this book:

Are you a person with strong religious beliefs?

Do you regularly attend a worship service?

Do you regularly (nearly daily) spend significant devoted time learning from God in the *whole word* (not just favorite sections) to better understand who God is and what his plan is on earth?

Do you spend regular time speaking with and listening to him throughout your day?

If the answer to the first two are *yes* and the last two are *no,* then you are a member of a *cult.* Or, you might as well be. If you believe what you have heard what sounds and *feels* right to you – you are following emotions and the teachings of man.

Your view of God is inadequate, incomplete, and idolatrous.

Because, in the words of Jesus and the Old Law – you are not engaging your *mind,* your God-given reason and comprehension, in your pursuit of the Holy One.

If you want to follow the One True Living God, you must spend time in conversation and thought with him each day – otherwise, you are a cult-member, or worse, an idolater. Or perhaps, an idolatrous cult-member.

If so, do not be angry with me.

Own it. And do not stay there!

We can only know the God that Elihu knew through knowing him, and that requires putting down the electronic device, turning off the television, and making an inviolate choice to sit down with God every day and learn from him through his written Word.

2.   Satan's Heart

Satan is a created being just like us – but he was made for a different purpose and realm. His domain was originally around the throne of God, as one who basked in God's glory and reflected that glory. He was a beautiful creature, and from what little Scripture tells us, he mistook his beauty for something to his own credit and led a rebellion against God.[214]

While in our times Satan has gained some sympathy and respect, the story of Job shows this to be misplaced and badly in error.

Even though Satan had been in the very presence of God in his fullest glory, his pride resulted in full-scale depravity. Even *he* could not comprehend the holiness, goodness, and love of God. And thus, he makes his wager that constituted slander against God. In effect, he contends that the Creator of all is not inherently worthy of loyalty – he is only handy because of the benefits he *might* confer.

Further, the ferocity of the attacks against Job should also *horrify us*. That any creature could hold such malice and contempt for a fellow created being should be absolutely disturbing. We hear of mass murderers killing, sexually abusing, and even eating their victims – and we wonder, *how could someone be so vile?*

In the story of Job, we find the answer.

Those who fail to seek God diligently and purposefully listen to him each day are likely to fall prey to the deceiver. Then, they may begin doing the very things he whispers to them.

Satan should not be underestimated. When he is allowed to act as he pleases, death, sorrow, suffering, and unspeakable cruelty are always the result.

But there is where we learn another lesson from this story; Satan should not be overestimated. As one close friend of Jesus noted:

He who is in you is greater than he who is in the world.[215]

Michael Youssef stated what should be our attitude toward Satan so well:

> *We need to know our enemy – to understand him, to outmaneuver him, to keep out of his reach, and to drive him away. But at the same time we should not get our priorities out of order. We should not pay Satan the compliment of thinking about him so much that he comes to dominate our lives. We need to be sober and vigilant, yet we also need to be oriented to the positive. We need to keep our eyes on Jesus, the author and finisher of our faith. For the closer we are to him, the more we appreciate and come to value the good things of God's kingdom, the more natural it will be for us to reject the devil's temptations and live in the Spirit.*[216]

As mentioned earlier, what was written long ago is written for our learning and encouragement. We must take Satan seriously and learn his strategies and modes of operating. The story of Job is a wide-open unadulterated look at what Satan *will do* if permitted.

That reality, of the extreme malice of Satan toward a good man, his family, his friends, his community, and his God *for no good reason* should drive us to seek the shelter of God and his truth *every day*.

3.   **Never let go of God**

God is the most worthy person in the universe to be loyal to. Job, in spite of his anger and harsh words, never lets go of his Lord. Job cannot understand what has happened, misinterprets what is going on, and makes some blasphemous accusations against the character and judgment of God.

But yet he holds on to his faith in his Creator.

Each of us must consider the evidence and decide whether or not the Bible is authentic and whether or not Jesus is who he claims to be. As the writer of Hebrews stated:

Now faith is the assurance of things hoped for, the conviction of things not seen.[217]

If you look at the Greek words for *assurance* and *conviction,* you find that the familiar but dated King James version got it right when the translators said:

*Now faith is the **substance** of things hoped for, the **evidence** of things not seen.*

Our faith is not some vague feelings-based idea that bring us comfort. We are to examine the Scriptures, the history, the textual consistency, and scientific evidence to determine whether or not *there is sufficient evidence and substance to the claims regarding the Christ.*

If we find sufficient evidence, then we need to agree to the Covenant God made. The most complete description of this covenant is found in the New Testament book of 2 Corinthians. Chapters 3 through 6 contain the mission of the Covenant believer.

But agreeing to a covenant with God has some very serious implications – it is intended that one who enters a covenant with God will never break it, except under the penalty of *death.* And indeed, to break away from God permanently will be the ultimate death.

But to cut to the main idea – we would all do well to emulate Job. He did not give up on God in the moment of trial. He was confused, hurting, and his view of God was skewed – but he held on with an amazingly tenacious grip. He fully intended to demand an explanation from God for the errors in judgment he discerned – but in the moment his vision of God was clarified, those questions seemed, well, idiotic.

Work now to decide whether or not God is worth following, then work daily to build a rock-solid faith that will stand the trials ahead.

4.   **God's Amazing Glory**

God's glory gives us eternal perspective.

Were you surprised at Job's *wonderful* confession in the storm – considering the magnitude of what he had lost?

The difference between knowing *about* God versus *knowing* God is what is vital. Probably all of us start with learning about God. We hear preaching, maybe sit in Bible class, and perhaps read the Bible or other spiritual literature on our own – and we begin to learn *about God.*

But if we are ever to have true joy and a rock-solid bulletproof faith in our Creator, we must increasingly see God more truly as he is. We must experience the majesty that is God – in order to make sense of life on this battleground that we call earth. The writer of the Hebrew letter states it boldly:

> *Without faith it is impossible to please him, for whoever would draw near to God must believe that he exists and that he rewards those who seek him.*

The old King James version stated that the rewards came to those who *diligently* seek him – and that is a faithful translation of the Greek word. This seeking is a diligent inquiry and a careful seeking – it is a worshipful act of passion.

Our seeking must be intentional and *driven* if we are to experience the transforming glory of God. We must deliberately develop a more accurate view of God through the disciplined use of our mind and reason.

We must prayerfully seek the face of God, and ask him to reveal himself to us as we are able to receive this reward.

Strive to discover the wonder of God that Job found in the whirlwind, the view of God that obscures every challenge and heartbreak.

Strive to develop the truest vision of the Almighty that *you would die for*.

5.   **God's Tight Grip on His Children**

Satan's attack on Job was an attack on God.

The attack failed.

If you are pursuing God diligently, and doing the work of the kingdom of Heaven out of your love for him – you too will find yourself in the crosshairs of Satan's weapons.

It is an intimidating thought. As we have seen, the devil is crafty and cruel. He is no one to be trifled with.

But if you are a child of the Almighty and the Christ is your brother, the attack on you *will be perceived by your Father as an attack on himself.* He will rally his forces, his angelic armies, and he *will win.*

We will see *his victory, his glory, and his mighty arm.*

The Apostle Paul speaks to this truth of the book of Job better than I can:

What then shall we say to these things? If God is for us, who can be against us? He who did not spare his own Son but gave him up for us all, how will he not also graciously give us all things? Who shall bring any charge against God's elect? It is God who justifies. Who is to condemn? Christ Jesus is the one who died – more than that, who was raised – who is at the right hand of God, who indeed is interceding for us. Who shall separate us from the love of Christ? Shall tribulation, or distress, or persecution, or famine, or nakedness, or danger, or sword? As it is written, 'For your sake we are being killed all the day long; we are regarded as sheep to be slaughtered.'

No, in all these things we are more than conquerors through him who loved us. For I am sure that neither death nor life, nor angels nor rulers, nor things present nor things to come, nor powers, nor height nor depth, nor anything else in all creation, will be able to separate us from the love of God in Christ Jesus our Lord.[218]

Satan's purpose and heartless desire in the attack on Job was to separate this lover of God *from God*. The Apostle Paul makes it clear – *it can't be done.*

In fact, in the entire book of Romans, there is only one condition of our potentially being lost once we come to Christ and sign on to the New Covenant. Is what I have come to call *the Proviso:*

Note then the kindness and severity of God: severity toward those who have fallen, but God's kindness toward you, provided you continue in his kindness. Otherwise you too will be cut off.[219]

In every attack of Satan, all we need to do is *hold on.* We choose to remain in the kindness and loving mercy of our Savior. Perfect behavior or response is not needed; our Savior is ready and willing to save as long as we do not purposely abandon him.

This resolution to never abandon God will not happen in a person of shallow faith. We must dwell in the Word, we must be talking to our Savior, and we must be in God's family, the church.

But if we have even just a partial view of our glorious God, we will never let go of him. If we even partially understand his great love, wisdom, power, and beauty, we can say as the Apostle Peter did when some casual followers were walking away:

> *Lord, to whom shall we go? You have the words of eternal life, and we have believed, and have come to know that you are the Holy One of God.*[220]

Peter had seen enough. While he would run away on the night of the crucifixion, I perceive that it was one of those Job-moments that God knew would happen. Peter needed to keep growing, and his denial of the Christ on the night of the betrayal was a *God-moment* designed to humble and enlighten Peter.

Peter would die for his faith later. But he would die *in Christ*.

You know what else?

We may not survive the attack of Satan either. At least not in the mortal sense.

The Apostle Paul shared his understanding of the nature of Satan's challenges in this way:

> *For me to live is Christ, and to die is gain. If I am to live on in the flesh, that means fruitful labor for me. Yet which I will choose I cannot tell. I am hard pressed between the two. My desire is to depart and be with Christ, for that is far better. But to remain in the flesh is more necessary on your account.*

If we, like Paul and Job, can catch a glimpse of the glory that is God, we too can see our *death* as a very *desirable benefit!* This world has its *very good* aspects. The Creator enjoys creating things of immense and immeasurable beauty. It is thrilling to live in this epic adventure and be of service to the God who loves us.

But then, in those moments when we see more clearly who God is, we realize as Paul so passionately stated that being *in the very presence of the Almighty will exceed the beauty and joy of every great moment we have ever known on earth.*

Our physical death is simply a graduation into an eternity filled with more glory, beauty, and love than we can currently comprehend.

To be in the full presence of the God who now (I pray for you that this describes you) holds you tightly in his grip – that is joy everlasting!

6.   Always Defend God

Elihu was the unnamed man on the ash heap. He wasn't important enough to be listed amongst the friends. He was young, inexperienced, and of no consequence in his village.

But we learn something from this young man.

It is always right to defend God.

Elihu doesn't claim to have everything figured out, he specializes in one truth:

God. Is. Awesome.

He sticks to what he knows. As the storm that God is riding in on approaches, his praise grows louder and more impassioned. As the thunder rattles Job's aching bones, Elihu's fevered praise of his Maker pounds the listeners with even more force.

God. Is. Awesome!

It is Elihu's theme. He is enthralled and captivated by the God that Job has demeaned. He, unlike the notable men, isn't sure why such bad things have happened to Job.

But he does know that our God is great. He does know that God listens. He does know that God speaks.

He chooses to speak out of turn and take a risk of losing any respect he may have. He chooses to defend God whatever it may cost him. May the Almighty give us the strength, courage, and conviction to do the same.

Always defend God.

7.   When Friends are Suffering, Show up and Shut up

The beautiful thing that Bildad, Eliphaz, and Zophar did for Job was just showing up and sitting quietly. This is a lesson God preserved for us in the story of Job. What they did not do so well was *listening.* They allowed their strongly held religious conviction that God was punitive to get in the way of listening to their suffering friend.

An argument ensued.

In the middle of grief what is needed most is not our pet theological ideas, no matter how strongly held – what is needed is compassionate empathy. Compassion literally means to *suffer with*. Suffering with someone, silently or with few words, is the good path.

We understand that even the strongest believer may not respond entirely appropriately – and from the wisdom of the story of Job, we understand that it is okay to let the sufferer vent.

But while they vent, stay off of God's throne. You are not qualified to sit there.

If in doubt be silent.

If in doubt, say, "I'm sorry."

If in doubt, say, "I don't know why."

Just show up.

So Much More than Suffering

The story of Job changed my life, and continues to change my life. My prayer is that this simple book will be a tool that God uses to change and encourage you.

The God who is revealed in this story is magnificent and beyond comprehension. When Elihu speaks, our hearts swell with the possibilities of God and his greatness!

Can Elihu's proclamations of God's beauty be true?

They are, and as Job noted once he *experienced* the glory, Elihu didn't even know a fraction of the beauty, power, and excitement available in the presence of the Creator.

The story of Job is the story of life. It is about suffering, patience, and confusion. It is about the problem of God. It speaks of the sociopathic nature of Satan. It shouts the unshakeable love of our Father in heaven.

It is a story to be pondered. The lessons are usable every day of our life with God.

It is a story of a God who is truly "too wonderful."

If we can see even a portion of his glorious majesty, all else fades from our view.

A truer view of God will transform our every moment, if we will seek to truly see him.

Seek the LORD while he may be found; call upon him while he is near.[221]

EPILOGUE

OH, THAT MY WORDS WERE WRITTEN – WOULD ANYONE READ IT?

If you are not overly familiar with the story of Job, there comes a point at which Job is complaining about God's mistreatment, and he makes a very ironic statement:

Oh that my words were written! Oh that they were inscribed in a book! Oh that with an iron pen and lead they were engraved in the rock forever![222]

Funny, isn't it? We are thousands of years removed from the conversation, and here we are having an extended examination together of all that Job said. But if you couldn't tell from all that you have read up till now – I likewise have a desire burning in my heart.

Oh that someone would read, meditate, and abide in the Word of God!

The Pew research group reports that about 24% of Americans have not read a book in the last year.[223]

Research by Lifeway Research found that while the "majority of churchgoers desire to honor Christ with their lives and even profess to think on biblical truths, a recent study found few actually engage in personal reading and study of the Scriptures."[224] The percentage of those believers who read the Scripture *daily* was 19 percent, about the same as those who read "rarely/never," which was 18 percent.[2253]

When I speak with so many believers, what I hear them say so often is, "My pastor said...," or "My preacher taught us...", but almost never, "I was reading Isaiah this morning and found...". We are, as an old mentor of mine use to say, "baby birds."

Christians too often are sitting in the comfortable little nest of their church family, and they sit eagerly with their "beaks" open while their preacher/pastor drops some predigested Bible down their throats.

No effort is required, just show up and swallow.

It is sad.

It is immature.

It is *dangerous.*

People who do not read do not think clearly or critically. They certainly cannot apply the whole counsel of God to their lives. Further, just because the words that are heard *sound right* and *make sense to me* doesn't really validate them as Scriptural truth. Even Satan can quote Scripture, as he did in the temptation of Jesus.[226] Just because your favorite pastor uses Scripture does not mean he is using it *correctly*.

For that matter, while you may enjoy the preaching you hear and think is *sounds right* – just know that you could probably go to any *false religion* and hear some convincing preaching there as well. If you do not know how to use your mind critically, and are regularly studying truth, your ability to discern error or heresy will be virtually nil.

The Joy of Armoring Up

Much has been said about technique of spiritual warfare over the past three decades. There are conferences, there are those who recommend that we "cast out demons in Jesus' name."

Perhaps there is value in all of this – but the temptation of Jesus shows a bit of a different value. The Savior's reply to every misquoted Scripture of Satan is, "It is written."[2274]

Since one of Satan's key strategies is *deception,* does it not follow that someone who knows very little of the Word of God can easily be deceived about what is true and right? If we are to be strong in our faith, if we are to resist the strategies and schemes of Satan, shouldn't we first and foremost be putting on the armor of God through dwelling in the Word daily?

In the Bible class I teach at my church on Sunday mornings, we call this our "armor-up" time. But I must share with you the truth about becoming a fully armored warrior of God.

First, it is very hard to establish a new habit. If you are waiting until the "spirit" moves you, you will likely *never* get there. Getting a habit established of spending quality time reading the Word (or what we call in our class, letting God speak to you) and conversing with God requires diligent effort. Satan will oppose you in this. His opposition is likely the primary reason you will never achieve this by *waiting for it to mysteriously happen.*

I heard on a podcast from one of my favorite preachers, Chip Ingram, the way in which he established the habit of daily time with God in his Word. He, like me, likes to eat. And so, realizing the vital necessity of feeding himself spiritually each day, he made an agreement with between himself and God; "No Bible, no breakfast."

He shared that it was hard for him at first, but once you get into the habit, you will find yourself so excited about it that you are eager to get out of bed – just in anticipation of what God is going to teach you that day.

I can personally share with you what this time has meant to me.

I was at one point an evolution-believing atheistic humanist. I was pretty proud of my amazing intelligence. I was living life my way, on my terms, and using my logic.

I nearly destroyed myself. At the same time I tried to disprove the Bible. It was a terrifying and wonderful experience.

But since that time, I have had a high respect for the eternal wisdom of God, and I joyfully anticipate his presence as we meet each day. I have times when I laugh out loud, and times when I cry. I have done my armor-up time on my back patio, in an airplane, and even in a hotel bar in Louisville, Kentucky. (The restaurant was crowded, so the hostess asked if I would mind sitting at the bar. I said no, spread out my Bible and journal and sat at the bar with God.) This habit, if you choose to establish it, will transform your life, your family, your friends, and your church.

Realize that we are bathed in a culture that continually distracts us and steals our time through electronic media. The smartphone or tablet you carry with you enslaves you with tiny hits of brain chemicals called dopamine—your time, your *life, is being stolen from you!* While we as blood-bought believers may *claim* that the Bible is the Word of God, it is clear that too many of us are worshipping our devices, and the good feelings they produce within us.

Get control of your devices.

Get control of your life.

If you want a simple plan, try the following:

1.   Eliminate all non-essential apps from your phone/tablet. This would be social media, games, and messenger programs such as Facebook messenger or Snap Chat. Turn your smartphone into a dumb phone as much as practical. Only keep programs essential for your work or survival.

2.   Put the plane in the hangar. As a career pilot I found this idea handy. Every night, about two hours before bedtime, I hook my phone up to a charger away from my bed. I get two hours to relax, connect with my wife, read, and eliminate the sleep disturbing device from my brain so that I can get some good rest. In the morning, I don't pick it up

until *after* I have had my "armor-up" time with God, talked with my wife, and relaxed over some coffee. Put the plane in the hangar as much as possible—do not worship it.

3.   Strive for face-to-face time with friends, in-person. Stop texting as much as possible. Texting is convenient, but time consuming and impersonal. I do a lot of calling now to hear the voices of my friends and family, and wherever possible, I arrange to meet with my besties. We need connection.

4.   When with your besties, keep the phone out of sight. Do not lay your phone on the table, even face down. Keep it out of sight and silent. Do not respond to the vibration if it happens; instead be fully present with the real person right in front of you. If you have a smart watch, when it fails, get a dumb watch. Every time that thing vibrates and you look away from the eyes of the person you are with, you are making a statement. Don't do it, and get rid of the smartwatch as soon as possible.

5.   Read real books. Read a real Bible. Stop doing digital as much as practical. There is a peace found in the printed word. There is the feel of the book, the positional awareness of where you are, and a better

ability for undistracted solitude and focus. Like I share with my friends, if you are reading a real printed Bible, if you get a notification, it is from the Holy Spirit instead of Uber Eats! Keep your devices away from you while reading if you can. Reading brings peace, develops your attention span, and helps you to grow exponentially in your wisdom (if you choose good literature).

6.   Choose healthy activities that make you feel good. If you have been enslaved by your electronic devices, make a list of things that you want to do and then put them on your schedule (get a real printed planner with room for note taking, good for your "armor-up" insights). Join a community choir, bowling league, take up bike riding, swimming, walking, running, or something *real*. Do good things that get you out of the house, with people, and that nourish your soul. Kick electronic addiction to the curb.

If you succeed, the joys of this daily armor-up time will draw you to that time every time. God will endow you with wisdom and discernment. People will seek you out for his wisdom. You may find yourself speaking to individuals or great crowds. You may write a book.

But your greatest joy will be learning of the awesome loving God who will not let us go. You will learn things "too wonderful, which I did not know."

Job wished for his words to be in a book.

God's desire is that you would read his.

ABOUT THE AUTHOR

Stephen K Moore is a writer, seminar speaker, and teacher of God's Word. His passion is to help others increase their enthusiasm in their daily walk with God. He has a Master's Degree in Marriage and Family Therapy and is integrally involved in the work of his church family in Dickson, Tennessee. He and his wife Anita have been married for thirty-three years and have four children and two sons-in-law.

For more information go to StephenMooreSpeaks.com or on Facebook @BeElihu

ENDNOTES

1   Coffman, J.B., 1993. *The Book of Job, vol. 1,* of *The James Burtram Coffman Commentaries – The Wisdom Literature, vol. 1.* Abilene: A.C.U. Press.

2   Job 1:9, New Living Translation, 2015, Tyndale House Foundation.

3   Job 1:7, English Standard Version, 2000, Crossway

4   Job 1:7, Ibid.

5   Job 1:8, ibid.

6   Job 1:9-10, New Living Translation.

7   Job 1:11, ibid

8   Henry, Matthew. *Job.* Matthew Henry Commentary on the Whole Bible (Complete). N.p. http://www/biblestudytools. Com/commentaries/matthew-henry-complete/job/.

9   Job 1:1-3, English Standard Version

10   Job 1:4-5, ibid

11   Job 1:5, ibid

12   Ibid, ibid

13   Ibid, ibid

14   Job 2:9, ibid

15   Ezekiel 18:23, English Standard Version

16   Genesis 1:31, ibid

17   Job 1:16, ibid

18   Job 1:2, ibid

19   Job 1:20, ibid

20   Job 1:22, ibid

21   Job 2:3, ibid

22   Job 2:4-5, ibid

23   Job 2:9, ibid

24   Job 2:10, ibid

25   Job 2:12, ibid

26   Job 2:13, ibid

27   Job 2:10, English Standard Version

28   Job 3:1, ibid

29   Job 3:20-23, ibid

30   Job 6:4, ibid

31   Job 7:13-19, ibid

32   Job 9:15-18, ibid

33   ibid

34   ibid

35   Job 9:22-24, ibid

36   Job 11:2-3, ibid

37   Job 9:27-29, ibid

38   ibid

39   Job 1:5, ibid

40   Job 9:30-31, 33, ibid

41   Job 10:2-3, ibid

42   Job 10:6-9, ibid

43   Job 10:20, ibid

44   Job 13:15-16, ibid

45   Koukl, G., 2013, Retrieved from https://www.str.org/articles/never-read-a-bible-verse#.W5ZV3NN95xg

46   Job 13:15, English Standard Version

47   Job 13:15-16, ibid

48   Job 16:7-14, portions, ibid.

49   Job 19:7, ibid

50   Ibid.

51   James 5:11, ibid

52   Exodus 20:7, ibid

53   Job 2:3, English Standard Version

54   Job 38:2-3, New Living Translation

55   Job 38:4-5, English Standard Version

56   Job 13:15, ibid

57   Job 13:22-24, ibid

58   Job 40:8, New Living Tranlation

59   Matthew 6:25, English Standard Version

60   Job 40:2, New Living Translation

61   Job 40:4-5, ibid

62   Job 42:2, English Standard Version

63   Job 42:3, ibid

64   Job 42:3, New Living Translation

65   Exodus 33:18, English Standard Version

66   Job 42.3, ibid

67   Exodus 33:19-20, ibid

68   Exodus 33:21-23, ibid

69   Job 43:4-6, ibid

70   Job 42:6, ibid

71   Job 8:4, ibid

72   Job 42:5, New Living Translation

73   Job 42:5-6, English Standard Version

74   Tozer, A.W. (1961). *The Knowledge of the Holy.* New York; Harper Collins

75   1 John 4:18, English Standard Version

76   Job 42:3, ibid

77   ibid

78   Romans 8:28, ibid

79   Job 42:2, ibid

80   Job 42:11, ibid

81   Job 2:5, English Standard Version

82   Job 38:2, ibid

83   Job 38:3, New Living Translation

84   Job 38:4-7, ibid

85   Job 38:21, ibid

86   Job 40:2, English Standard Version

87   Job 40:8-9 ibid

88   Job 2:3, ibid

89   Job 42:7-8, ibid

90   Psalm 2:1-4, ibid

91   Job 32:1, ibid

92   Psalm 103:8-14, ibid

93   Job 42:3, ibid

94   Job 42:12, ibid

95   John 1:16, ibid

96   Malachi 3:6, ibid

97   2 Samuel 24:14, ibid

98   Psalm 111:10, ibid

99   Hebrews 12:7-8, ibid

100   Job 1:8

101   Romans 5:3-6

102   Matthew 10:16-22, sections, New Living Translation

103   Matthew 10:28-31, ibid

104   Job 42:2, English Standard Version

105   2 Chronicles 14:11, New Living Translation

106   2 Chronicles 14:8, ibid

107   2 Chronicles 14:12

108   Isaiah 55:8-9

109   Ephesians 6:13, English Standard Version

110   1 Kings 19:4

111   1 Kings 19:9, 13

112   I Kings 19:14

113   The story is found in 1 Kings 18:17-40

114   Wiliamson, P.B., *General Patton's Principles for Life and Leadership,* 1988, p. 197, Tucson, Management and Systems Consultants, Inc.

115   1 Kings 19:15-18, selections

116   Luke 15:11-18, New Living Translation

117   Matthew 28:20

118   Luke 1:28-38

119   Luke 1:34

120   Luke 1:38

121   Luke 1:49

122   Jeremiah 29:12-14

123   Romans 12:2

124   Job 42:3

125   Job 42:3

126   Job 32:2-5, English Standard Version

127   Job 38:2, ibid

128   Job 42:7, ibid

129   Romans 9:20-21 ibid

130   Job 33:9-11, ibid

131   Job 33:12, ibid

132   Isaiah 6:1, ibid

133   Isaiah 6:5, ibid

134   Job 33:14, ibid

135   Retrieved from https://albertmohler.com/2016/01/20/the-scandal-of-biblical-illiteracy-its-our-problem-4/

136   Retrieved from https://www.technologyreview.com/the-download/610045/the-average-american-spends-24-hours-a-week-online/

137   Retrieved from https://www.theatlantic.com/technology/archive/2018/05/when-did-tv-watching-peak/561464/

138   Job 33:14, English Standard Version

139   Job 33:15-17, ibid

140   Job 33:30, ibid

141   Job 42:3, ibid

142   Job 42:5-6, ibid

143   Job 33:26-28, ibid

144   Job 42:6, ibid

145   Job 32:2, ibid

146   Matthew 15:25, ibid

147   Isaiah 63:1-2, ibid

148   Proverbs 3:5, ibid

149   Job 34:5-9, English Standard Version

150   1 Samuel 17:26, English Standard Version

151   1 Samuel 17:33, ibid

152   1 Samuel 17:36-37, ibid

153   1 Samuel 17:39, ibid

154   Job 34:10, ibid

155   Job 34:11, New Living Translation

156   Exodus 3:14, ibid

157   Job 34:14-15, ibid

158   Job 10:20, ibid

159   Job 19:11, ibid

160   Courtois, S., Werth, N., Panne, J., Paczkowski, A., Bartosek, K., & Margolin, J. (1999). *The big black book of Communism: Crimes, terror, repression.* Cambridge, MA: Harvard University Press.

161   Job 36:2, English Standard Version

162   Job 36:3-4, ibid

163   Luke 1:46ff, ibid

164   Genesis 1:31, ibid

165   Psalm 73, sections, New Living Translation

166   Job 21:7-9, English Standard Version

167   Job 73:16-20, New Living Translation

168   Luke 13:34, English Standard Version

169   Job 36:13-14, ibid

170   Daniel 4:28-37, ibid

171   Daniel 4:37, ibid

172   Job 36:15, New Living Translation

173   Acts 10:24, ibid

174   Job 36:18, English Standard Version

175   Job 36:24, ibid

176   Job 36:27-32, ibid

177   Job 37:1, 5, ibid

178   Mayer, S. (2009). *Signature in the cell: DNA and the evidence for intelligent design.* New York; Harper Collins

179   Job 37:1, 5, English Standard Version

180   Proverbs 30:18-19, New Living Translation

181   Job 37:14, ibid

182   Psalm 19:1-4, ibid

183   Job 37:21-24, ibid

184   Job 37:24, ibid

185   Psalm 111:10, English Standard Version

186   Matthew 14:27 is one example, and God says this throughout the Bible. He desires

a loving relationship, ibid

187   2 Corinthians 4:16-18, ibid

188   Job 35:9. English Standard Version

189   Joshua 3:15, ibid

190   Joshua 4:21-23, ibid

191   Joshua 4:24, ibid

192   Watts, I. (1707). Public domain

193   Job 36:24-26, English Standard Version

194   Roberts, T., Wiles, J., & Wiles, T. (2017). *Conquer Series.* Stuart, FL; Kingdom-Works Studios.

195   Luke 1:19, ibid

196   1 Corinthians 11:27-30, ibid

197   John 19:30, ibid

198   1 Peter 2:24, ibid

199   Romans 5:6-11, ibid

200   Romans 5:8, ibid

201   Job 2:11, New Living Translation

202   Job 2:13, ibid

203   Proverbs 17:27-28, ibid

204   Job 8:4, ibid

205   Job 11:6, ibid

206   Isaiah 29:13, English Standard Version

207   Job 42:7, ibid

208   Job 42:5-6, English Standard Version

209   Tozer, A.W., (1961). *The knowledge of the Holy.* New York; HarperCollins

210   Psalm 104:1-2, 31-34, English Standard Version

211   Romans 15:4, ibid

212   Mark 12:31, ibid

213   Moreland, J.P., (1997). *Love God with all your mind: The role of reason in the life of the soul.* Colorado Springs; NavPress

214   The majority of what is known about Satan is found in Ezekiel 28:11-19 and Isaiah 14:12-15.

215   1 John 4:4, English Standard Version

216   Youssef, M. (1984). *Know your real enemy.* Nashville; Thomas Nelson

217   Hebrews 11:1, English Standard Version

218   Romans 8:31-39, ibid

219   Romans 11:22, ibid

220   John 6:68, ibid

221   Isaiah 55:6, ibid

222   Job 19:23-24, ibid

223   Pew Research, retrieved from http://www.pewresearch.org/fact-tank/2018/03/23/

who-doesnt-read-books-in-america/

224   Lifeway Research, (2014). *Study: Bible engagement in churchgoers' hearts, not always practiced.* Retrieved from https://www.lifeway.com/en/articles/research-survey-bible-engagement-churchgoers?carid=jhowe-stetzer-bible-20120913

225

226   Matthew 4, English Standard Version

227

www.ingramcontent.com/pod-product-compliance
Lightning Source LLC
Chambersburg PA
CBHW080956120626
46546CB00010B/2924